Dedicated to America's Korean War veterans,
with gratitude for their sacrifices.

Publishers • Lawrence Siegel & Art Worthington
Designers • Peter Hess & Marguerite Jones
Writing & Research • Beverly Cohn
Facilitator • Pamela Thomas

www.FLICKBACK.com
(800) 541-3533

Contents

Arts
&
Entertainment

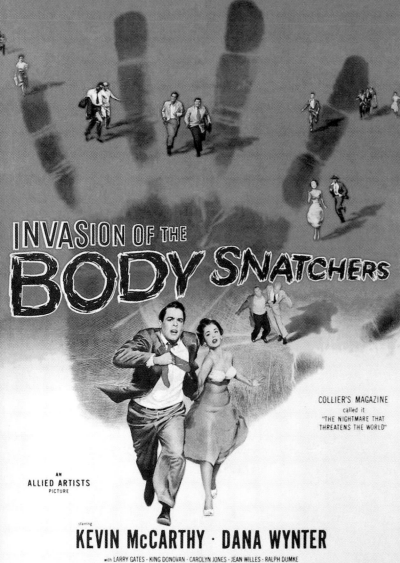

Movie audiences are chilled by the alien-occupied "pod people" in the science fiction classic, **Invasion of the Body Snatchers**, which spawns several remakes and comes to be regarded by some as a representation of Cold War paranoia.

Movies

James Dean

died tragically in a 1955 road accident while driving his Porsche 550 Spyder near Cholame, California—the same year which saw the release of his films *East Of Eden* and *Rebel Without A Cause*. 1956 finds "Rebel" continuing as a top-grosser, and the posthumous release of *Giant* helps cement Dean's legacy as one of his generation's most compelling actors.

What's Playing AT THE MOVIES

Alexander The Great

Anastasia

Anything Goes

Around The World In 80 Days

Baby Doll

Bigger Than Life

BUS STOP

CAROUSEL

Diane

FORBIDDEN PLANET

Forever Darling

Friendly Persuasion

Gaby

GIANT

HIGH SOCIETY

I'll Cry Tomorrow

IT'S A DOG'S LIFE

LEASE OF LIFE

Lust For Life

Meet Me In Las Vegas

Moby Dick

Picnic

Richard III

Romeo and Juliet

Somebody Up There Likes Me

Teahouse Of The August Moon

The Benny Goodman Story

The Bottom Of The Bottle

the court jester

The Harder They Fall

The Invasion Of The Body Snatchers

The King And I

The Ladykillers

The Last Wagon

The Littlest Outlaw

The Man In The Gray Flannel Suit

The Man Who Never Was

The Naked Sea

The Opposite Sex

THE RAINMAKER

The Searchers

THE SEVENTH SEAL

THE SOLID GOLD CADILLAC

The Ten Commandments

Too Bad She's Bad

WAR AND PEACE

WRITTEN ON THE WIND

You Can't Run away From It

8

9

RKO PANTAGES

28TH ANNUAL
AWARDS PRESENTATIONS
OF THE ACADEMY OF MOTION PICTURE ARTS AND SCIENCES

Hollywood's Pantages Theater

Fans gather outside the Pantages Theatre hoping to catch a glimpse of their favorite stars.

*The star-studded crowd includes past Oscar winner **Frank Sinatra** and **Jimmy Cagney**, a contender for this year's Best Actor award.*

"WONDERFUL!" ...Time

"A TRIUMPH!" ...Louella Parsons

"SUPERB, WARM, RICH!" ...Cue

"A FINE FILM...A GEM!" ...Li

HECHT-LANCASTER present

"MARTY"

starring ERNEST BORGNINE and BETSY BLAI

Story and Screenplay by PADDY CHAYEFSKY
Directed by DELBERT MANN · Produced by HAROLD HECHT
Associate Producer: Paddy Chayefsky · Released thru UNITED ARTISTS

Ernest Borgnine, *congratulated by host*
Jerry Lewis, *is named Best Actor of the year*
for his performance in Marty *and receives his*
award from **Grace Kelly**.

Ernest
Borgnine

Hosts The Oscar® Presentations

THEATRE

THE
ROSE TATTOO
is the boldest story of love you
have ever been permitted to see!

THE
ROSE TATTOO
is marked with the passionate
impact of Tennessee Williams,
Pulitzer Prize Winning Author
of "A Streetcar Named Desire."

THE
ROSE TATTOO
stars Burt Lancaster and Anna
Magnani, winner of this year's
New York Film Critics Award!

BURT LANCASTER · ANNA MAGNANI
in
Hal Wallis'
production of
TENNESSEE WILLIAMS'
THE ROSE TATTOO

VISTAVISION

Jerry Lewis *presents*
the Oscar for Best Actress
to Italian star **Anna**
Magnani *for her role in*
"The Rose Tattoo."

Marisa Pavan accepts on
Miss Magnani's behalf.

Anna Magnani

THE ACADEMY AWARDS

Oscars® Presented in 1956

BEST PICTURE
MARTY

BEST ACTOR
ERNEST BORGNINE,
Marty

BEST ACTRESS
ANNA MAGNANI,
The Rose Tattoo

BEST DIRECTOR
DELBERT MANN,
Marty

BEST SUPPORTING ACTOR
JACK LEMMON,
Mr. Roberts

BEST SUPPORTING ACTRESS
JO VAN FLEET, *East Of Eden*

BEST SONG
"LOVE IS A MANY SPLENDORED THING"

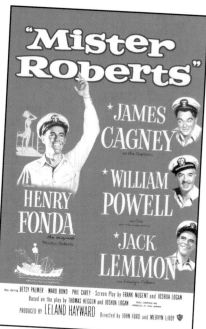

1956 Favorites *(Oscars® Presented in 1957)*

BEST PICTURE
AROUND THE WORLD IN 80 DAYS

BEST ACTOR
YUL BRYNNER, *The King And I*

BEST ACTRESS
INGRID BERGMAN, *Anastasia*

BEST DIRECTOR
GEORGE STEVENS, *Giant*

BEST SUPPORTING ACTOR
ANTHONY QUINN, *Lust For Life*

BEST SUPPORTING ACTRESS
DOROTHY MALONE,
Written On The Wind

BEST SONG
"WHATEVER WILL BE, WILL BE"
(QUÉ SERSÁ, SERSÁ)

Yul Brynner

12

TOP STARS of '56

Lauren **BACALL**

Marlon **BRANDO**

Gary **COOPER**

Kirk **DOUGLAS**

Henry **FONDA**

Glenn **FORD**

Cary **GRANT**

Audrey **HEPBURN**

William **HOLDEN**

Danny **KAYE**

Burt **LANCASTER**

Dean **MARTIN** & Jerry **LEWIS**

Marilyn **MONROE**

Kim **NOVAK**

Frank **SINATRA**

James **STEWART**

Robert **TAYLOR**

John **WAYNE**

BORN IN 1956 ★
LISA HARTMAN
BLACK • DEBBY
BOONE • DELTA
BURKE • DAVID
COPPERFIELD • BO
DEREK • CARRIE FISHER •
ANDY GARCIA • MEL GIBSON
• TOM HANKS • LA TOYA
JACKSON • JUDGE REINHOLD
ERIC ROBERTS • PAULA ZAHN

Tom Hanks

NEW STARS of '56

Pier **ANGELI**

Yul **BRYNNER**

Joan **COLLINS**

Tony **CURTIS**

Diana **DORS**

Anita **EKBERG**

Rock **HUDSON**

Jeffrey **HUNTER**

Tab **HUNTER**

Shirley **JONES**

Janet **LEIGH**

Jack **LEMMON**

Gina **LOLLOBRIGIDA**

Vera **MILES**

Aldo **RAY**

Sal **MINEO**

George **NADER**

Sheree **NORTH**

Rod **STEIGER**

Natalie **WOOD**

Dana **WYNTER**

William Holden and Natlie Wood

★ **Rita Hayworth** Settles Nine-Month Feud With Columbia Pictures.

★ A.F.L. Film Union Demands Boycott Of Non-Union Film *Daniel Boone*.

★ Revised MPAA Censorship Code Revised To Discourage Racial Slurs And The Glorification Of Crime.

★ The Motion Picture Industry Revises And Relaxes Its Moral Code For The First Time Since Its Creation In 1930.

★ The "Cameo" Appearance Debuts In Mike Todd's *Around The World In 80 Days*.

HOLLYWOOD BIDS A FOND FAREWELL

JACK COHN (67) was a co-founder of Columbia Pictures.

Danish-born Actor **JEAN HERSHOLT** (69) enjoyed a career spanning 50 years as a film star.

CLARENCE E. MULFORD (73), was the creator of "Hopalong Cassidy."

Cartoonist, **ALEXANDER GILLESPIE RAYMOND** (46), was creator of "Flash Gordon."

Television

EMMY AWARD WINNERS

TOP 10 TV Shows

1. The $64,000 Question
2. I Love Lucy
3. The Ed Sullivan Show
4. Disneyland
5. The Jack Benny Show
6. December Bride
7. You Bet Your Life
8. Dragnet
9. The Millionaire
10. I've Got A Secret

BEST SERIES
(half hour or less)
The Phil Silvers Show

BEST SERIES
(one hour or more)
Caesar's Hour

BEST NEW SERIES
Playhouse 90

BEST SINGLE PROGRAM
"Requiem For A Heavyweight"
Playhouse 90

BEST ACTOR
DRAMATIC SERIES
Robert Young
Father Knows Best

BEST ACTRESS
DRAMATIC SERIES
Loretta Young
The Loretta Young Show

BEST COMEDIAN
Sid Caesar
Caesar's Hour

BEST COMEDIENNE
Nanette Fabray
Caesar's Hour

BEST SUPPORTING ACTOR
CARL REINER
Caesar's Hour

BEST SUPPORTING ACTRESS
PAT CARROLL
Caesar's Hour

BEST ACTOR
SINGLE PERFORMANCE
JACK PALANCE
"Requiem For A Heavyweight"
Playhouse 90

BEST ACTRESS
SINGLE PERFORMANCE
CLAIRE TREVOR
"Dodsworth"
Producers' Showcase

BEST MALE PERSONALITY
PERRY COMO

BEST FEMALE PERSONALITY
DINAH SHORE

BEST NEWS COMMENTATOR
EDWARD R. MURROW

BEST ORIGINAL
TELEPLAY WRITING
(one hour or more)
ROD SERLING
"Requiem For A Heavyweight"
Playhouse 90

Keenan Wynn, Jack Palance and Ed Wynn
Playhouse 90, CBS
"Requiem for The Heavyweight"

SOAPS!
Get Out Your Hankies, Ladies

The first soap operas to be televised daily hit the air with the debut of *The Edge Of Night* and *As The World Turns* on CBS-TV.

Good Night, David—

Good Night, Chet

NBC-TV teams up Chet Huntley and David Brinkley for a nightly news show after their impressive co-anchoring of the Democratic Convention in Chicago.

WILL THE REAL ? PLEASE STAND UP

Tom Poston and **Kitty Carlisle** head celebrity panelists on the new quiz show *To Tell The Truth*. The goal is for the mystery guests to lie so convincingly that the panel believes their alleged identity.

Due To Poor Ratings, Mr. Television, Milton Berle, Loses His Time Slot For The First Time In Eight Years And His Announces Retirement.

CBS—TV Begins Airing NFL Games On Sundays.

The first *Popeye The Sailor* Cartoons Air on TV.

Nat "King" Cole Becomes The First Black Performer To Headline A Prime-Time Television Program.

Nat "King" Cole

1956 ADVERTISEMENT

WHERE DOES
A WOMAN'S SYMPATHY
LEAVE OFF—AND
HER INDISCRETION
BEGIN?

"Years from now,"
Laura was saying softly,
"when you talk about this—
and you will—be kind . . ."

From the sensational stage success that ran 91 weeks . . . and
starring the players who created the original Broadway roles

M-G-M presents in CINEMASCOPE and METROCOLOR

Tea and Sympathy

Deborah Kerr · John Kerr

with

Leif Erickson · Edward Andrews

screen play by Robert Anderson · based on the play by Robert Anderson · directed by Vincente Minnelli · produced by Pandro S. Berman · An M-G-M picture

21" PICTURE TUBE*

*OVERALL DIAMETER—254 SQUARE INCHES OF VIEWABLE PICTURE

Big as life. Even the lowest priced RCA Victor Big Color set gives a huge 254 square inches of viewable picture—crisp and clear in black-and-white or Color.

All the colors of life. RCA Victor Big Color TV gives Color so natural, so alive—you have to see it to believe it. It's a completely new experience in home entertainment.

Practical and dependable. Big Color TV service is low-cost—RCA Factory Service Contracts are available in most areas, but only to owners of RCA Victor TV sets.

See Color every night—even a child can tune it. (Shown) The *Aldrich* (21CS781) in limed oak grained finish. $495.

"LIVING COLOR" AT $495 IS NOW BEST TV BUY—IT'S LIKE 2 SETS IN 1

New RCA Victor Big Color is *the* TV for thrifty families. Now you can enjoy Color plus black-and-white in one TV set!

Here is double-value Color TV at the lowest price in history. Now you and your family will see every program *exactly* as it is broadcast. The big Color shows in breathtaking "Living Color"—all regular programs in sharp, clear black-and-white.

You see them easily with new "Color-Quick" tuning—so simple a child can do it. Turn two knobs and the screen blossoms out in Color.

You have your choice of 10 Big Color models—from table model to full-door console in contemporary or traditional styling.

See "Living Color" with your own eyes at your RCA Victor dealer's soon. Ask him about easy budget terms on any Big Color set—your present TV may even cover the down payment!

Manufacturer's nationally advertised VHF list price shown subject to change. UHF optional, extra. **At your service:** RCA Victor Factory Service Contracts from $39.95 (90 days).

RCA VICTOR
RADIO CORPORATION OF AMERICA

RCA PIONEERED AND DEVELOPED COMPATIBLE COLOR TV

Like 2 sets in 1 because it's RCA Victor *Compatible* Color. Color shows in Color—all others in black-and-white. This is today's common-sense investment in TV.

Radio

TOP NETWORK RADIO PROGRAMS

SUMMER 1956

◇◇◇ Best Of Groucho ◇◇◇
◇◇ Truth Or Consequences ◇◇
◇◇ Godfrey's Talent Scouts ◇◇
◇◇◇ Hambletonian Stakes ◇◇◇
◇◇◇ News From NBC ◇◇◇
◇◇◇◇ Gangbusters ◇◇◇◇
◇◇◇◇ Treasury Agent ◇◇◇◇
◇◇ True Detective Mysteries ◇◇

OTHER FAVORITES

Aunt Jenny	Helen Trent
House Party	My True Story
Nora Drake	Our Gal Sunday
Road Of Life	Second Mrs. Burton
Young Dr. Malone	

RADIO WORLD BIDS A FAREWELL

FRED ALLEN, radio entertainer whose radio program "Allen's Alley" drew an estimated 20 million listeners, dies at 61 of a heart attack.

TOP 10 RECORDS

1 **Don't Be Cruel**
   Elvis Presley

2 **Great Pretender**
   The Platters

3 **My Prayer**
   The Platters

4 **Wayward Wind**
   Gogi Grant

5 **Whatever Will Be, Will Be**
   (Qué Será Será)
   Doris Day

6 **Heartbreak Hotel**
   Elvis Presley

7 **Lisbon Antigua**
   Nelson Riddle

8 **Canadian Sunset**
   Hugo Winterhalter

9 **Moonglow and Theme From "Picnic"**
   Morris Stoloff

10 **Honky Tonk**
   Bill Doggett

FRANKIE LYMON
Is Rock 'N' Roll's First Teenage Star At Age 13.

POPULAR MUSIC

The Hits

Blueberry Hill	Just Walking In The Rain
Blue Suede Shoes	Long Tall Sally
Chain Gang	Love Me Tender
Flying Saucer (Parts I & II)	Memories Are Made Of This
Green Door	More
Hot Diggity/ Jukebox Baby	No, Not Much
Hound Dog	Poor People Of Paris
I Almost Lost My Mind	Rock And Roll Waltz
I'm In Love Again	Roll Over Beethoven
I Want You, I Need You, I Love You	Singing The Blues
	Standing On The Corner

BILL HALEY & HIS COMETS
Lose Favor With The Younger Audiences.

The King Of Swing Swings With The King

Thailand's King Phumiphol Aduldet teams up with Benny Goodman for an impromptu jazz session.

"Rock And Roll" Dance Becomes Popular.

Rock 'N' Roll
Revolutionizes The Recording Industry, Catapulting Black Artists Onto The Charts.

Annie Mae Bullock, 16, Changes Her Name To **TINA TURNER** On Joining Ike Turner's Band.

NAT KING COLE
Attacked During Concert In Birmingham, Alabama.

Lionel Hampton Dazzles French Audience In Jazz Concert.

Don't Step On My Blue Suede Ratings

ELVIS PRESLEY

Gains In Popularity And Makes His First Television Appearance Introduced By Tommy and Jimmy Dorsey.

A Record TV Audience Of An Estimated 54 Million People Tunes In To Watch Elvis Sing *Hound Dog* And *Love Me Tender* On The *Ed Sullivan Show.*

RECORDING STARS OF TOMORROW

| Johnny Cash | James Brown | Eydie Gorme |
| Coasters | Diamonds | Roy Orbison |

A NOTE OF FAREWELL

TOMMY DORSEY, "Sentimental Gentleman of Swing", dies at 51, leaving the legacy of "the greatest all-around dance band of them all." Frank Sinatra, vocalist for the band in the 40's, credited his vocal phrasing to Mr. Dorsey's extraordinary trombone musicianship.

ART TATUM, American jazz pianist, dies at 46.

DANNY RUSSO, composer of "Toot, Toot, Tootsie Goodbye", 71.

ALBERT VON TILZER, composer of "Take Me Out To The Ball Game", "I'll Be With You In Apple Blossom Time", 78.

ISHAM JONES, composer of "It Had To Be You", "I'll See You In My Dreams", 63.

classical music

PULITZER PRIZE
ERNEST TOCH
"Symphony No. 3"

Vienna State Opera Gets New Musical Director – Herbert von Karajan.

Austria Celebrates Mozart On Bicentennial.

Opera Premiere: Douglas Moore, The Ballad Of Baby Doe." Gian Carlo Menotti Debuts His Opera, "The Unicorn, The Gorgon And The Manticore" In Washington, D.C.

William Bergama's Opera "The Wife Of Martin Guerre" Opens In New York.

Maria Callas Debuts At The Metropolitan Opera In Bellini's "Norma".

Maria Callas

- **LILY PONS** Celebrates 25th Anniversary Of Metropolitan Opera Debut.

- Self-Exiled Spanish Cellist, **PABLO CASALS**, Announces He Will Make His Home In Puerto Rico.

- **MATTIWILDA DOBBS** Debuts As Gilda In "Rigoletto" With The New York Metropolitan Opera, Becoming The Third Black Singer To Be Featured At The Metropolitan And The First To Sing A Non-Black Romantic Lead.

dance·dance·dance·dance·dance·

New Ballet: Humphrey Searle, "Noctambules"

Ballerina Margot Fonteyn Is Appointed Dame Commander Of The Order Of The British Empire.

Sadler's Wells Ballet Renamed The Royal Ballet.

ON·OUR·

·TOES·ON·OUR·TOES·ON·OUR·

BROADWAY OPENINGS

theatre

Bernstein's Musical Comedy "Candide" Opens In New York.

PLAYS

A Hatful Of Rain ◆ Auntie Mame ◆ A View From The Bridge ◆ Bells Are Ringing ◆ Desk Set ◆ Fallen Angels ◆ Li'l Abner ◆ Long Day's Journey Into Night ◆ Look Back In Anger ◆ Middle Of The Night ◆ No Time For Sergeants ◆ Richard III ◆ The Chalk Garden ◆ The Great Sebastians ◆ The Lark ◆ The Matchmaker ◆ The Most Happy Fella ◆ Tiger At The Gates ◆ Waiting For Godot ◆ Will Success Spoil Rock Hunter?

Terence Rattigan's "Separate Tables" Opens In New York.

"The Iceman Cometh" By Eugene O'Neill Opens At Circle-In-The-Square In New York.

on BROAD

Alan Jay Lerner & Frederick Loewe Open "My Fair Lady" In New York.

Julie Andrews, center

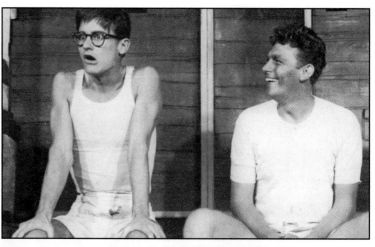

No Time For Sergeants
From left: Roddy McDowall and Andy Griffith

WAY

A View From The Bridge
*From left: Gloria Marlowe, Van Heflin
and Eileen Heckart*

Fallen Angels
Nancy Walker

Candide
Irra Pettina

Bells Are Ringing
*Judy Holliday and
Peter Gennaro*

PORGY & BESS
PLAYS LENINGRAD

The first American musical troupe to ever visit Leningrad performs "Porgy & Bess," receiving a 10-minute standing ovation from a wildly enthusiastic audience.

TONY AWARDS

DRAMATIC ACTOR:
Paul Muni, *Inherit The Wind*

DRAMATIC ACTRESS:
Julie Harris, *The Lark*

PLAY:
The Diary Of Anne Frank

MUSICAL ACTOR:
Ray Walston, *Damn Yankees*

MUSICAL ACTRESS:
Gwen Verdon, *Damn Yankees*

MUSICAL:
Damn Yankees

Brecht's Berliner Ensemble Visits England.

BERTOLT BRECHT, prolific playwright including *The Threepenny Opera* and *Mother Courage And Her Children*, dies at 58.

A Streetcar Named...
I'm Outta Here

Ater attending several performances of "A Streetcar Named Desire" featuring Tallulah Bankhead's loud interpretation of the Blanche Dubois character, author Tennessee Williams is so pained he leaves town to avoid hearing anything else about the nightly spectacle.

Pulitzer Prize

Frances Goodrich & Albert Hackett

The Diary of Anne Frank

New York Drama Critics
CIRCLE AWARDS

BEST PLAY
The Diary Of Anne Frank,
Frances Goodrich & Albert Hackett

BEST FOREIGH PLAY
Tiger At The Gates,
Christopher Fry

BEST MUSICAL
My Fair Lady,
Alan Jay Lerner & Frederick Loewe

Let Doris and Roy Pinney, famous husband-wife photographer team, help you choose

The Right Ansco "Great Year" Camera

for Father, Mother, Daughter, Son

"Looks very slick indeed," says Doris, picking up an Anscoflex II. "A woman really would like this. Your subject shows up so clearly in the big viewing window. You can see what you're getting. No guesswork.

"Because a woman is home, she's able to take pictures on important occasions like birthdays. She's there and able to watch. So every woman should have a camera she can operate quickly and easily. It *is* quick and easy with this fixed-focus camera; you don't have to be a mechanical whiz to work it.

"The same reasons that make this a good camera for a woman, make it a fine choice for boys and girls, or for any beginner. The other fixed-focus camera, the Readyflash, is very easy to use, too and a good size for taking with you."

With a man in mind, Roy Pinney points out that "The 35mm camera is becoming increasingly a color camera." He adds, "The more seriously a man regards color photography, the more you are justified in giving him the very finest 35mm camera Ansco makes.

"You'll notice they all have fine fast lenses and shutters, and many up-to-date features that help a man get better pictures. But even the simpler, less costly models are quite capable and take really fine color pictures."

If he has a feeling for fine cameras—precision-built 35mm camera at a popular price! Superb *f* 3.5 lens, action shutter to 1/300. Lens-coupled range-view finder. Thumb-lever film transport. **Super Memar f 3.5, $69.50**

For a true hobbyist—first camera in America to feature new Light Value System, which many say is the photographic system of the future. *f* 3.5 lens; shutter speeds to 1/500; coupled rangefinder. 35mm. **Super Regent, $89.50**

If he has outgrown all but the best—newest 35mm camera in America, one of the finest ever to carry Ansco name, priced far lower than you'd expect! *f* 2 lens. Speeds to 1/500. Coupled rangefinder. **Super Memar f 2, $119.50**

Christmas morning . . . as only Anscochrome can picture it!

The camera that understands a beginner . . . and vice versa—Anscoflex II with big viewing window, built-in close-up lens and cloud filter. Plus leather case, flash unit and bulbs, film, travel kit. Worth $33.75. **Anscoflex II Outfit complete, $27.95**
Anscoflex I Outfit, $22.95

Wonderful "Stocking Gift"

. . . or when you want to make it a remembrance more substantial than a greeting card . . . a roll or two of Ansco All-Weather Pan black-and-white film. Or better still, Anscochrome color film!

For a youngster—for anyone who wants pictures the easy way—Readyflash is the ready-set, all-fun, no-fuss camera! Plus flash unit and bulbs, Ansco film . . . all in handy travel kit. Worth $15.80. **Readyflash Outfit complete, $11.95**
Readyflash camera alone, $6.95

If he's ready to graduate to color pictures—the 35mm Memar with color-corrected *f* 3.5 lens, plus leather case, flash unit, color film . . . all in a handsome travel kit. Worth $61.20. **Memar Outfit complete, $56.25**
Memar camera alone, $39.50

Only with 3-times-faster Anscochrome . . .

Color pictures so charmingly true-to-life

Christmas is red and green, gold and silver. Christmas is a tree and a feast and the family come together.
Christmas is the time of times for the great *new* color pictures you get with Anscochrome . . . the super-speed successor to traditional color films.
Three-times-faster Anscochrome pictures Christmas in its true colors . . . the warm, vibrant colors of life itself. *Ansco, A Division of General Aniline & Film Corp., Binghamton, N. Y.*

The super-speed successor to traditional color film
. . . available in 35mm, 120, 620, 828, 16mm movie and sheet sizes.

art

Primitive Painter Grandma Moses Turns 96.

Emilio Greco's Statue of Pinocchio, Honoring The Author Of The Classic Tale, Carlo Lorenzini, Wins Over 82 Others In A Sculpture Competition In Ancona, Italy.

Young British Painters Swing Back To Realism And Are Dubbed "The Kitchen Sink School."

Claude Monet's Water Lily Paintings Are Acquired By The Museum Of Modern Art And The Art Institute Of Chicago, Thrusting The Great French Impressionist Painter Into Prominence.

The Frank Lloyd Wright Designed Los Angeles Municipal Art Gallery Is Dedicated And Construction On His Guggenheim Museum Begins In New York.

Richard Lippold's Commissioned Piece, "Variation Within A Sphere, No. 10: The Sun" Goes On Exhibition In New York's Metropolitan Museum of Art. The Piece Is Constructed With More Than Two Miles Of Wire And 14,000 Hand-Welded Joints.

Sam Francis, 32-Year Old Ex-GI, Becomes The Most Well Known American Painter In Europe, Specializing In Exploration In The Quality Of Light.

VENICE BIENNALE PRIZES

PAINTING: Jacques Villon (80 Year Old French Cubist)
SCULPTURE: Lynn Chadwick (Great Britain)
DRAWING: Aldemir Martins (Brazil)

NEW PAINTINGS

John Bratby ......*"A Painter's Credo"*
Lynn Chadwick ..."*Teddy Boy And Girl*"
Bernard Buffet ...."*Self-portrait*"

NEW SCULPTURE

Barbara Hepworth *"Orpheus"*

Prehistoric Art Discovered In Caves In Dordogne, France

An Original "Madonna And Child"
By Leonardo da Vinci Valued At $1 Million Is Found In
A New York Antique Shop.

"Composition #3" By Russian Pioneer Abstractionist
Wassily Kandinsky, Painted In 1914, Is Finally Shown.

With The Growing Interest In American Paintings, Museum Directors Have Turned To The American Impressionists, Buying Such Works As Childe Hassam's "Church At Old Lyme, Conn.," Maurice Prendergast's "Sunset And Sea Fog" And John Twachtman's "Fishing Boats At Gloucester."

London Critics Give Less Than Hospitable Reception To Modern U.S. Art Exhibition On Display At The Tate Gallery, Finding Works By Jackson Pollock, Clyfford Still, Willem de Kooning, Mark Rothko And Robert Motherwell Disquieting And Nightmarish.

Painter Charles Burchfield Lauded By Critics And Dubbed The Greatest Living U.S. Watercolorist Despite His Opinion That Most People Are Bored Or Indifferent About Nature, The Subject Of His Works.

New York's National Academy Of Design Awards The Benjamin Altman Figure Painting Prize To Morton Roberts For His Work Entitled "Bar And Grill."

The United States Participates In The 28th Venice Biennale With An Exhibition Assembled By The Art Institute Of Chicago Entitled "American Artists Paint The City" Consisting Of Works By Edward Hopper, John Marin, Stuart Davis And Jackson Pollock.

PASSINGS

Jackson Pollock, Pioneer Abstract Expressionist, Dies At 44 In An Automobile Accident.

Maurice Utrillo, French Painter, Dies At 71.

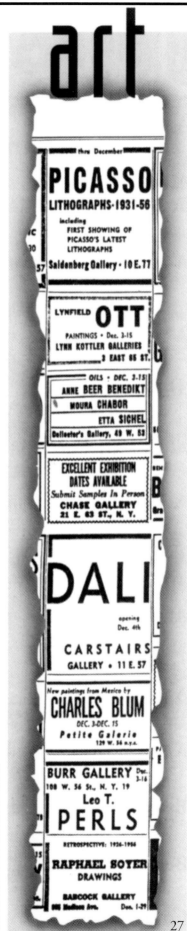

books

A Charmed Life
MARY MCCARTHY

A Family Party
Ten North Frederick
JOHN O'HARA

A Historian's Approach To
Religion
ARNOLD TOYNBEE

A Season To Beware
WILLIAM DUBOIS

A Single Pebble
JOHN HERSEY

A Walk On The Wild Side
NELSON ALGREN

Adonis And The Alphabet
ALDOUS HUXLEY

All Honorable Men
DAVID KARP

All The Kingdoms
Of The Earth
HOKE NORRIS

Amrita
R. PRAWER JHABVALA

Anglo-Saxon Attitudes
ANGUS WILSON

Bang The Drum Slowly
MARK HARRIS

Boon Island
KENNETH ROBERTS

Comfort Me With Apples
PETER DE VRIES

Diamonds Are Forever
IAN FLEMING

Don't Go Near The Water
WILLIAM BRINKLEY

Essays On The Sociology
Of Culture
KARL MANHEIM

Field Of Vision
WRIGHT MORRIS

Freedom Or Death
NIKOS KAZANTZAKIS

Helen Keller: Sketch
For A Portrait
VAN WYCK BROOKS

H.M.S. Ulysses
ALISTAIR MACLEAN

Howl And Other Poems
ALLEN GINSBERG

Imperial Woman
PEARL BUCK

Lady Sings The Blues
BILLIE HOLIDAY

Lucy Crown
IRWIN SHAW

Men And Power, 1917
LORD BEAVERBROOK

Notes Of A Native Son
JAMES BALDWIN

Nuni
JOHN HOWARD GRIFFIN

O Beulah Land
**MARY LEE
SETTLE**

PULITZER PRIZES

BIOGRAPHY

Talbot F. Hamlin
Benjamin Henry Latrobe

FICTION

MacKinlay Kantor
Andersonville

POETRY

Elizabeth Bishop
"Poems, North And South"

books

Obscenity And The Law
NORMAN ST. JOHN-STEVAS

Paper Dolls
LAURA BEHELER

Peyton Place
GRACE METALIOUS

Profiles In Courage
JOHN F. KENNEDY

Seize The Day
SAUL BELLOW

Speak To The Winds
RUTH MOORE

The Atlantic Battle Won
SAMUEL ELIOT MORISON

The Color Curtain
RICHARD WRIGHT

The End Of The Track
ANDREW GARVE

The Horse Soldiers
HAROLD SINCLAIR

The King Of Paris
GUY ENDORE

The Last Hurrah
EDWIN O'CONNOR

The Malefactors
CAROLINE GORDON

The Man Who Studied Yoga
NORMAN MAILER

The Man Who Was Not With It
HERBERT GOLD

The Marble Orchard
MARGARET BOYLEN

The Ninth Wave
EUGENE BURDICK

The Nun's Story
KATHRYN HULME

The Organization Man
W.H. WHYTE

The Outsider
COLIN WILSON

The Quiet American
GRAHAM GREENE

The Search For Bridey Murphy
MOREY BERNSTEIN

The Theme Is Freedom
JOHN DOS PASSOS

The Tribe That Lost Its Head
NICHOLAS MONSARRAT

The Young Lincoln
STERLING NORTH

This Is Our World
LOUIS FISCHER

Walk Through The Valley
BORDEN DEAL

What I Think
ADLAI STEVENSON

PASSINGS

GEORGE TERRY DUNLAP, Co-Founder Of Grosset & Dunlap, Dies At 92.

A.A. MILNE, Creator Of "Winnie the Pooh," Dies At 74.

H.L. MENCKEN, Author And Editor, Dies At 75.

Oh-h-h! those '56 OLDSMOBILES!

with new *Jetaway*

HYDRA-MATIC

ALL THE *Flow* OF FLUID . . . ALL THE *Go* OF GEARS!

1956 SUPER 88 HOLIDAY SEDAN

The secret of the smoothness *is in the* second *coupling!*

Paired with the Rocket T-350 for the smoothest action ever!

Liquid-smooth and lightning-quick! Oldsmobile's new Jetaway Hydra-Matic gives you the flashing action of "going" gears plus the velvet smoothness of *two* fluid couplings. The result is almost an air-borne feeling—quiet, swift and incredibly smooth. In fact, the dazzling new Oldsmobile will outperform, outgo, outstrip any Rocket model before it . . . *by far!* And in appearance, the new Olds is a standout, too. With inspired new Starfire styling—bold new airfoil grille—sweeping new body lines—a *daring, different* look from every angle! Visit our showroom soon . . . see the cars that are out ahead to *stay ahead* . . . new Rocket Oldsmobiles for '56!

NOW ON DISPLAY AT YOUR OLDSMOBILE DEALER'S

OLDSMOBILE

In The News

Seventeen nuclear weapons are detonated on Bikini and Enewetak Atolls in the Pacific as part of the U.S. military's **Operation Redwing**. The series includes the *Cherokee* test, the first airdrop of a thermonuclear weapon.

Politics *and* World Events

The Russians Give and Take

The Soviet Union begins divesting some European territories of her troops. Brandenburg in East Germany sees a good-faith withdrawl of Russian troops, and in Finland, Russia relinquishes its naval base, ending an 11-year occupation. However, in Hungary, a patriots' revolt against the Russian forces unleashes a chain of events closely watched by the entire world. More than 25,000 Hungarians are killed in the Budapest revolt with 30,000 wounded. By December more than 20,000 Hungarian refugees enter United States.

East Germany: first contingent of Russian troops demobilize.

RED TROOPS

EAST GERMANY

Military observers from Western Allied Headquarters arrive in Brandenburg to witness a token withdrawal of Red forces from East Germany as part of Russia's withdrawal proposal.

Involved in the operation is the removal of 89 obsolescent planes and the first contingent of 50,000 troops that Russia announces it will demobilize.

A Russian photographer records the evacuation which is part of an overall reduction of Russian troops.

WITHDRAW...

FINLAND TAKES OVER IT'S NAVAL BASE

DAILY NEWS

Russian and Finnish officers salute each other, bringing an end to an 11-year occupation by Russian forces.

Photographers capture this historic moment.

With the signing of the treaty relinquishing the Russian naval base on Finnish soil, Finnish soldiers arrive to take over the 220-square mile base.

Every trace of Russian occupation is destroyed and all Scandinavia breathes easier as Red guns cease to dominate the Baltic.

As the Finns enter their regained territory, they find a looted and sabotaged installation. Power houses are dismantled and gun emplacements are destroyed.

Hungary's

VALIANT FIGHT FOR FREEDOM

Emblems of Red tyranny come down for 10 glorious days as Hungarian patriots struggle against 20 Russian armored divisions.

The struggle pits raw courage and rifles against tanks.

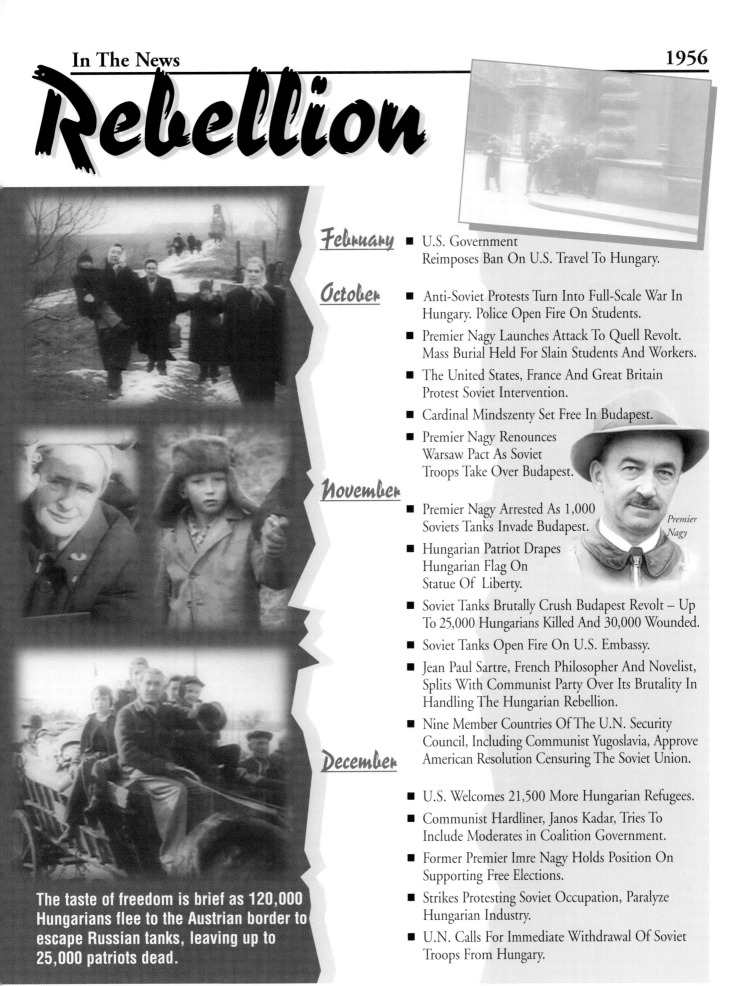

Rebellion

February
- U.S. Government Reimposes Ban On U.S. Travel To Hungary.

October
- Anti-Soviet Protests Turn Into Full-Scale War In Hungary. Police Open Fire On Students.
- Premier Nagy Launches Attack To Quell Revolt. Mass Burial Held For Slain Students And Workers.
- The United States, France And Great Britain Protest Soviet Intervention.
- Cardinal Mindszenty Set Free In Budapest.
- Premier Nagy Renounces Warsaw Pact As Soviet Troops Take Over Budapest.

November
- Premier Nagy Arrested As 1,000 Soviets Tanks Invade Budapest.
- Hungarian Patriot Drapes Hungarian Flag On Statue Of Liberty.
- Soviet Tanks Brutally Crush Budapest Revolt – Up To 25,000 Hungarians Killed And 30,000 Wounded.
- Soviet Tanks Open Fire On U.S. Embassy.
- Jean Paul Sartre, French Philosopher And Novelist, Splits With Communist Party Over Its Brutality In Handling The Hungarian Rebellion.
- Nine Member Countries Of The U.N. Security Council, Including Communist Yugoslavia, Approve American Resolution Censuring The Soviet Union.

December
- U.S. Welcomes 21,500 More Hungarian Refugees.
- Communist Hardliner, Janos Kadar, Tries To Include Moderates in Coalition Government.
- Former Premier Imre Nagy Holds Position On Supporting Free Elections.
- Strikes Protesting Soviet Occupation, Paralyze Hungarian Industry.
- U.N. Calls For Immediate Withdrawal Of Soviet Troops From Hungary.

Premier Nagy

The taste of freedom is brief as 120,000 Hungarians flee to the Austrian border to escape Russian tanks, leaving up to 25,000 patriots dead.

Beautiful new way to bring back the colorful moments of your life.....life-size

Files and safeguards slides! Aluminum magazines keep precious slides in perfect, indexed order. Individual metal frames protect them from dirt, smudges, dog-earing. Your fingers never touch the transparencies.

Spectacular picture quality! A powerful, 4-inch wide-angle lens gives you big-as-life pictures that let the whole family enjoy the show—even in a small room.

NEW ARGUS AUTOMATIC PROJECTOR $59.50
complete with carrying case, automatic slide changer, slide editor and 36-slide magazine

You've photographed the big moments of your life in color. Now relive them—big as life and just as colorful—with this new Argus Automatic!

A new, advanced optical system delivers more light through the wide-angle lens to give you pictures uniformly bright and clear, from corner to corner.

And your slides are so easy to show. A quick push-pull of the operating handle positions each slide for perfect viewing, returns it to the magazine in order, and automatically advances the next slide.

A convenient Slide Editor lets you pre-view slides before you file them in the magazine. And a powerful yet silent blower keeps projector and slides cool—even during long showings.

To see your color slides in a beautiful new light, see the all-new Argus line of 300-Watt Projectors at your dealer's now.

Standard model, with non-automatic operation, $37.50. New Remote-Control Power Unit for any Argus Automatic, runs the show by push-button from anywhere in the room, $24.50.

Easy to use...Easy to own...That's Argus!
Most dealers offer convenient credit terms

BRITAIN AND U.S. ISSUE JOINT STATEMENT

President Eisenhower and Britain's Prime Minister, Sir Anthony Eden, conclude three days of talks in Washington on world problems with the issuance of a joint warning to the people of Asia and Africa on the dangers of economic and political help from the Soviet Union.

The two world powers further pledge joint action to defend the peace in the Middle East.

THE NAVY of

AMERICA TAKES REVOLUTIONARY STEP FORWARD

The U.S.S. Boston, America's first guided missile cruiser, pictured in maneuvers off Cuba. Ship and missile are designed for each other in what engineers call an integrated weapons system.

From below deck magazines, the missiles, with lethal capabilities, are positioned on launching racks where a full salvo can be aimed and fired in seconds and guided to the target while in flight.

TOMORROW

IN NAVAL WARFARE AND THE NATION'S DEFENSE

Guided missiles with increased range are added to the underseas arsenal and the submarine becomes a more formidable weapon of counterattack on enemy coasts.

The atomic submarine *Nautilus* passes all tests with flying colors, cruising submerged a distance equivalent to circling the globe.

41

The Symbol that links the bounty of the sea to your pantry shelves

Fish from the waters of Maine and California . . . from far-away Alaska and the Gulf of Mexico . . . come to your pantry today with extra flavor and nutrition because of the can and a symbol you probably seldom notice.

The symbol is a trade-mark—a small oval on the ends of cans made by American Can Company.

Back of it is Canco's belief that the can is more than a container; it's a way of helping you live better . . . more conveniently . . . for less money.

Back of it, too, is Canco's motto "Can do," and the *spirit of cooperation* that makes this motto work.

BEHIND THIS SYMBOL ARE THE SERVICES OF CANCO'S "CAN DO" MEN. HERE'S HOW THEY HELP BRING YOU TASTIER CANNED FISH.

AS ANY FISHERMAN KNOWS, the quicker fish is prepared after catching, the better the flavor. To help the industry preserve flavor and cut catch-to-can time, Canco was first to develop high-speed machinery to fill cans and close under vacuum.

FOOD CHEMIST L. G. GERMAIN is one of the many specialists who help the fishing industry produce better products. Faced with tough problems and great opportunities, Canco's researchers and service people have always answered "Can do"!

CANCO "Can do"...*that's the spirit of* American Can Company

ARGENTINEANS RALLY

Several hundred thousand people mass in the Plaza Congreso to demonstrate their faith in the current regime with cries of **"Libertad."**

After a decade of rule by dictator Juan Peron, the crowd jeers his name as speaker after speaker condemns his iron rule of the Republic.

TURBULENT ELECTION IN KOREA

THE MOST TURBULENT ELECTION IN KOREA'S YOUNG HISTORY AS A REPUBLIC SWINGS INTO HIGH GEAR WITH PUBLIC INTEREST AT A HIGH PITCH.

President Rhee *(right poster)* faces strong opposition for the first time from Democratic party leader, P.H. Shinicky.

Shinicky makes his first campaign speech to an enthusiastic crowd. Later, he suffers a fatal heart attack leaving Rhee virtually unopposed.

With the sudden death of Shinicky, tension mounts as his followers take to the streets, some of whom storm President Rhee's palace.

MARSHAL TITO of Yugoslavia arrives in Paris for a state visit. Accompanied by his wife, Tito is welcomed by a corps of French government officials.

EXTREME SECURITY measures are taken as France has not forgotten the assassination of King Alexander of Yugoslavia 22 years ago. Guards are alerted as Tito arrives at the Palais de L' Elysée.

TITO VISITS PARIS

President Coty decorates Marshal Tito with the Military Cross for actions against Hitler.

Will you really <u>enjoy</u> your *retirement*...
or barely scrape along?

You have probably given a lot of thought to how you would *like* to spend your time after retirement . . . maybe you have even figured how much income you would need to do the things you want.

Is the amount you can presently count on enough? Think how much peace of mind an *extra* $100 a month would contribute!

The question is: "Where is this *extra* $100 coming from?" Maybe you expect to save it. If so, it would take $30,000, invested safely at 4%, to provide a gross income of $100 monthly. Few people have the means to do this.

However, there is a simple, safe and sure way of providing for *extra* retirement income—a Metropolitan Retirement Program. This also provides Life insurance protection for your family in case something should happen to you before retirement. The cash and loan values in the policy can be used as nest eggs in the event of unforeseen contingencies.

Your Metropolitan Representative will show you how, step by step, you can provide for financial security during your retirement years. He will estimate the amount of retirement income Social Security will contribute, and help you review the possible income from your present policies in the light of your future retirement plans and needs. You might also ask him about a Family Income rider to give *added* protection to your family.

Any Metropolitan Representative will welcome this chance to show that . . .

Metropolitan service is
> **as local as Main Street . . .**
>> **as close as your phone**

Metropolitan Life Insurance Company
(A MUTUAL COMPANY)
1 MADISON AVENUE, NEW YORK 10, N. Y.

COPYRIGHT 1956—METROPOLITAN LIFE INSURANCE COMPANY

Salute to Ike

President addresses diners in 53 cities

Madison Square Garden in New York sets the pace in the national SALUTE TO IKE dinners across the nation. 0,000 Republicans gather and eat $100 box dinners to help swell campaign coffers for the coming election.

The President and Mrs. Eisenhower acknowledge the applause of his supporters.

TONITE N Y & N J
SALUTE TO IKE
HOLLYWOOD ICE REVUE
NIGHTLY THRU JAN 30
MAT SAT & SUN

MARINES EMBARK FOR NEAR EAST TROUBLE SPOT

As the threat of war looms in the Near and Middle East, the Second Battalion of the Eighth Marines embarks for the Mediterranean on six ships of the Atlantic Fleet.

Even as the Marines deploy, new violence erupts in Cyprus, North Africa and Palestine.

EGYPT PARADES ITS ARSENAL OF RED WEAPONS

Russia's new foreign minister, Dmitri Shepilov, architect of the arms deal, observes the proceedings.

EGYPT FLEXES ITS MILITARY MUSCLE WITH A DISPLAY OF ARMS NEWLY ACQUIRED FROM RUSSIA AND ITS SATELLITES.

The parade, which climaxes a 3-day celebration of the withdrawal of the last British troops from the Suez, is presided over by newly elected president Abdel Nasser, spearhead of the Arab bloc of nations.

WAR OVER SUEZ

In a dramatic sequence of events, the Suez Canal, lifeline of Europe, becomes a cause of war.

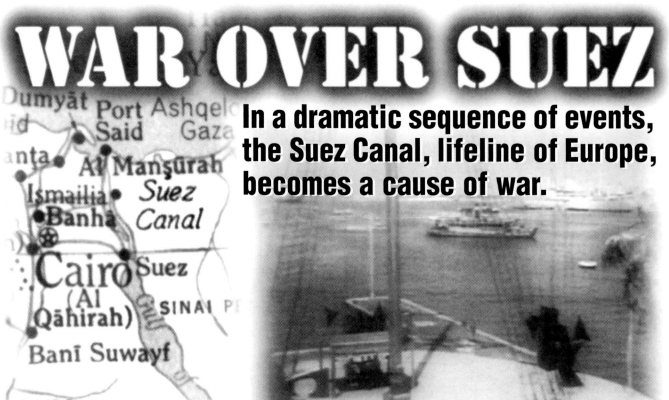

JUNE	• Britain ends 72-year occupation of the Suez Canal Zone.
JULY	• Egypt's President Nasser announces nationalization of the Suez Canal Company – seizing full control of the Canal.
AUGUST	• United States, France and Great Britain hold discussions on the Suez Canal. Great Britain mobilizes forces.
	• Egypt announces willingness to discuss the Suez only after Great Britain and France pull out.
	• Nasser agrees to five-nation mission to discuss the Suez.
	• Britain grants France permission to station troops on Cyprus.
SEPTEMBER	• Egypt assumes full control of Suez Canal using all Egyptian employees – war threatened.
OCTOBER	• 15 member nations formally inaugurate Suez Canal Users Association.
	• Morocco and Tunisia recall their ambassadors to France in protest over action in the Suez.
	• President Eisenhower assures nation that U.S. will not get involved in Middle East.
	• Britain, France and Israel move on Suez Canal. French and British planes bomb Egyptian airport and military installations near Suez. President Nasser vows Egypt will fight any foreign intervention.
NOVEMBER	• Israeli troops capture Gaza strip, seizing control of Sinai. Golda Meir claims Gaza strip is part of Israel.
	• In an overwhelming majority (65-1), U.N. Assembly calls for withdrawal of foreign forces.
	• Suez operation ends after intense pressure from the United Nations.
DECEMBER	• British and French troops evacuate from the Suez.

PRESIDENT ABDEL NASSER ANNOUNCES SEIZURE OF THE CANAL BY EGYPT.

ISRAELI TROOPS STRIKE DOWN THE SINAI PENINSULA TO WITHIN A FEW MILES OF THE CANAL AND WITHIN DAYS, EGYPTIAN TROOPS ARE COMPLETELY ROUTED.

BRITAIN AND FRANCE STAGE A

Airborne troops quickly follow and establish a beachhead at the entrance to the Canal.

The debris and chaos of bombing greet the Anglo-French forces as they enter the conquered cities.

JOINT SEA AND AIR INVASION

As the occupation proceeds, world opinion against the invasion is mobilized. At the United Nations, the invasion is branded "aggression" and a ceasefire is ordered.

To implement the decision, Secretary General Dag Hammarskjold flies to Egypt for preliminary negotiations.

The United Nations emergency police force is born.

The police force is jubilantly welcomed as it takes up its task in Egypt.

With this decisive action, the United Nations merits the confidence of President Eisenhower.

"In the past, the United Nations has proved able to find a way to end bloodshed. We believe it can and that it will do so again."

IT'S A LANDSLIDE EISENHOWER/NIXON

DAILY

Stevenson

THE REPUBLICAN CONVENTION meets in San Francisco and their choice by overwhelming acclamation is President Eisenhower.

Adlai Stevenson, former governor of Illinois, becomes the standard bearer for the Democratic party at its convention in Chicago.

FOR TICKET

Republican supporters gather in Times Square to await election returans.

Jubilant Eisenhower and Nixon greet their supporters in this historic election – the biggest land-slide victory since Franklin D. Roosevelt beat Alfred M. Landon in 1936.

Step in (it's easy to do).

THE FAIRLANE TOUCH THROUG

1956 FORD *Fairlane*

enjoy

AND THROUGH

Every Detail of the beautiful new Fordor Victoria says "Fairlane." Its smart Style-Tone and Single-Tone exteriors are a joy to behold. And its Luxury Lounge interiors are the last word in fine-car living.

No matter which selection strikes your fancy and meets your needs, you enjoy the utmost in good taste. Each new interior is color-keyed throughout—upholstery, carpeting and trim—to harmonize with whichever exterior color combination you choose.

Fresh new ideas are everywhere! There's a two-tone Thunderbird-type control panel, a harmonizing-color steering wheel, color-keyed carpeting, two-tone seat upholsteries in easy-to-clean, richly grained vinyls and smart patterned nylons, modern quilted-vinyl door panels . . . all beautifully crafted. Here, indeed, is fine-car living in the Fairlane manner.

❖ Fidel Castro, Exiled Student Leader, Accused Of Leading Cuban Rebels In Uprising.

❖ Sudan Proclaimed Independent Republic.

❖ Islam Becomes State Religion Of Egypt.

❖ First National Assembly Election Held In Viet Nam With Pro-West Diem Regime Winning.

❖ Socialist Guy Mollet Becomes French Premier.

❖ The 20th Congress Of The Communist Party Of The Soviet Union Officially Signals End of Stalinism And Return To Leninism.

❖ Tunisia Abolishes Polygamy, Amends Divorce Laws In Favor Of Wives And Grants Voting Rights To Women Over 21.

❖ Pakistan Becomes First Islamic Republic.

❖ Stalin Denounced By Khrushchev—Reforms Begin In U.S.S.R.

❖ West Germany Bans Communist Party And Reinstates Military Service.

❖ Luis A. Somoza Elected President of Nicaragua, Succeeding His Father, Anastasio.

❖ President of Nicaragua, General Anastasio Somoza, Victim Of Assassin's Bullet.

❖ Somalia Holds First National Elections.

❖ Golda Meir Replaces Moshe Sharett As Foreign Minister Of Israel.

❖ Egyptian President Nasser Proclaims End Of Martial Law And Censorship Of The Press In Effect Since The Overthrow Of King Farouk In 1952.

❖ King Mahendra, The World's Only Hindu Monarch, Is Crowned In Nepal.

❖ Japan And USSR End State Of War.

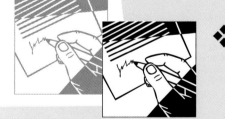

❖ Mutual Defense Pact Against Israel Signed By Syria And Lebanon.

❖ France Grants Independence To Its Two Protectorates In North Africa— Tunisia And Morocco.

Time-saver

Calling out of town? Here's a helpful hint: calls go through twice as fast when you call by number.

A good place to keep a list of the numbers you call is in an attractive Blue Book. You can get one at the Bell Telephone business office. It's free.

You'll find it handy to use. And a real time-saver, too.

LONG DISTANCE RATES ARE LOW	
Here are some examples:	
New York to Philadelphia	40¢
Seattle to Portland, Ore.	50¢
Cincinnati to St. Louis	75¢
Boston to Baltimore	85¢
Atlanta to Cleveland	$1.00

These are the Station-to-Station rates for the first three minutes, after 6 o'clock every night and all day Sunday. Add the 10% federal excise tax.

BELL TELEPHONE SYSTEM

all **3** for the price of TV alone!

- television
- phonograph
- hi-fi radio

AM OR AM/FM

MODEL 4RF84M

Olympic

world's leader in combinations

QUALITY VALUE FOR 21 YEARS

AFFILIATE OF UNITRONICS CORPORATION

Why settle for TV alone? Now, with Olympic you get giant-size TV...plus hi-fi automatic 4-speed phonograph...plus hi-fi radio...all in one luxury set...all for virtually the same price as an ordinary TV set alone. See these top-quality, value-packed combinations, table models, and consoles at your Olympic dealer today! 132 beautiful models in all...styled to fit every decor — traditional, modern, provincial and Chinese. Also — hi-fi radio-phonograph consoles from $149.95*

*SLIGHTLY HIGHER SOUTH AND WEST

OLYMPIC RADIO & TELEVISION
34-75 38th Avenue, Long Island City 1, N.Y.

☐ *Send me free literature on Olympic 3-Way combinations and hi-fi.*
☐ *Send me name of nearest Olympic dealer.*

Name_____

Address_____

City_____ Zone____ State____

PROTEIN

GIVES DOGS THAT TRIM, LITHE LOOK

If there's one thing your dog needs—for trim, lively good health—it's protein, *high-quality* protein. And that's what Gro-Pup has plenty of—about twice as much high-quality protein as most canned dog foods. Protein for firm flesh and muscle—Protein for vigorous health. Whatever else you feed—be sure to include Gro-Pup, the high-protein dog food, daily.

GRO-PUP
High Protein
DOG FOOD

GRO-PUP

HIGH-PROTEIN DOG FOOD

➤ President Eisenhower Names Citizens' Board To Monitor The Activities Of The CIA As Well As Other Security Gathering Agencies.

➤ President Eisenhower Authorizes Sale Of Uranium For Production Of Atomic Power Domestically And Abroad For Non-Military Use.

➤ George Meany Recommends To Democratic Platform Committee Federal Minimum Hourly Wage Be Raised To $1.25 And Tax Cuts For The Lower-Income Bracket.

➤ Test Pilot Killed As World's Fastest And Highest Altitude Airplane—U.S. Air Force's Bell X-2—Crashes.

➤ Russia Leads In H-Bomb Planes.

➤ Senator John F. Kennedy Is Edged Out Of Presidential Ticket As Democrats Name Senator Estes Kefauver As Adlai E. Stevenson's Running Mate.

➤ Soviet Complaints Lead To U.S. Halting The Launching Of Weather Balloons.

➤ U.S. Air Force Radar Detection Platform Designed To Scan The Atlantic Ocean For Aircraft Is Installed Off Of Cape Cod, Mass.

➤ Senator John F. Kennedy Appeals To Democrats To End Party Dissension That Could Lead To More Victories For The Republicans.

➤ Women In Congress Reaches Sixteen — A Record High.

BATTLES FOR DESEGREGATION

ALABAMA

Despite the protests by angry and hostile mob, Autherine Lucy becomes first African-American to be admitted to the University Of Alabama. The University then votes to suspend her because of demonstrations over her admission. She is later expelled because of charges she made against the University.

115 People Indicted By Montgomery, Alabama Grand Jury For Alleged Involvement In 11-Week Boycott Of Bus System.

Roy Wilkins in press conference with Autherine Lucy and Thurgood Marshall, director and special counsel for NAACP Legal Defense and Education Fund.

Martin Luther King, Jr. Convicted In Montgomery, Alabama State Court On Charges of Illegally Conspiring To Boycott Segregated Buses.

Segregation Of Public Transportation Declared Unconstitutional By U.S. Supreme Court.

Governors Of Georgia, Mississippi, South Carolina And Virginia United In Opposition Of Supreme Court's Ban On Racial Segregation In Public Schools. Virginia Supports Segregation By Funding Private Schools.

Students Seeking To Attend An Integrated High School In Sturgis, Kentucky, Have The Way Cleared For Them By National Guard Soldiers With Fixed Bayonets.

U.S. Supreme Court Affirms Ban On Segregated Public Schools.

University of Florida Ordered By Supreme Court To Admit Black Student To Its Law School.

Alabama State Court Bars The NAACP.

CLINTON HIGH SCHOOL KNOXVILLE, TENNESSEE

Tennessee National Guard Called In To Stop Riots Over Admission Of 12 Black Children in Clinton – Nine Students Admitted.

University of Alabama book burning.

United Nation's Secretary General Dag Hammarskjold Reports Israeli-Egyptian Cease-Fire Agreement.

 The Soviet Union Releases Poland's Wladyslaw Gomulka And Restores The Polish Army.

 Battle For Algiers Begins.

Eisenhower Rejects Soviets' Proposed 20-Year Treaty Of Friendship. Soviet Premier Bulganin Urges Ike to Reconsider.

DOUGLAS MACARTHUR II NAMED U.S. AMBASSADOR TO JAPAN.

Vice-President Nixon Delivers Letter From President Eisenhower To Generalissimo Chiang Kai-shek Confirming U.S. Support Of Nationalist China.

 Eisenhower Issues Statement Reaffirming U.S. Friendship With Great Britain And France.

PASSINGS

ALBEN BARKLEY,
U.S. Vice President 1949-1953, dies at 78.

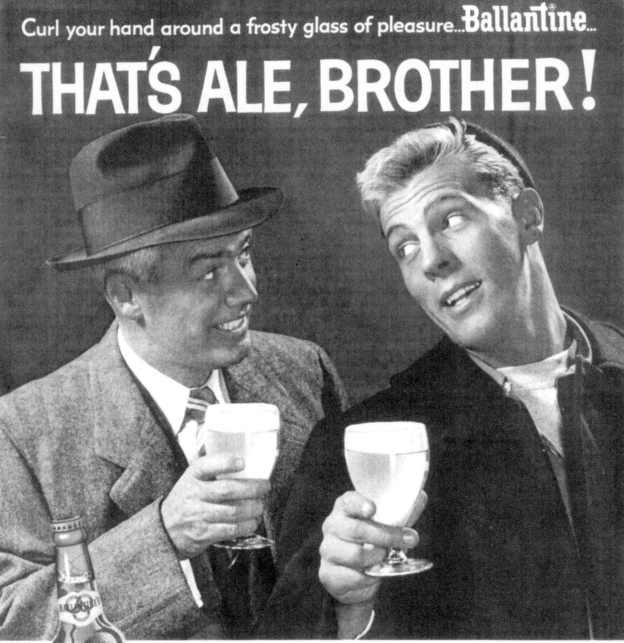

People

Monaco's Prince Rainier III *weds American actress* Grace Patricia Kelly *in a storybook wedding covered by 1,700 press, radio, TV and newsreel reporters.*

HOLLYWOOD'S MOVIE QUEEN SAILS OFF TO BECOME A PRINCESS

People

Surrounded by well-wishers and the press, Grace Kelly gets ready to board the S.S. Constitution for her trip to Monaco.

America wishes Grace bon voyage and a life-time of happiness.

THE WORLD'S MOST ELIGIBLE BACHELOR TAKES A BRIDE

All the world focuses on the tiny kingdom of Monaco as this storybook country prepares for Prince Rainier's marriage to American film queen Grace Kelly.

A wildly enthusiastic crowd gathers to greet the ship carrying the soon-to-be Princess Grace.

Prince Rainier III kneels next to Grace Patricia Kelly in the Roman Catholic St. Nicholas Cathedral in Monte Carlo after a civil ceremony the previous day.

HONEYMOONERS PRINCE RAINIER AND

The Prince and his famous movie queen bride make their way to their box for a day at the bullfights.

The festivities begin with the traditional grand march of the matadors and picadors.

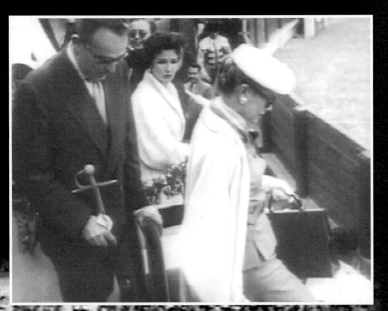

RINCESS GRACE ATTEND A BULLFIGHT

The opening ceremony receives royal approval.

Princess Grace is moved by the action in the ring as the bull gores the horse.

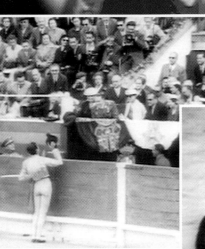

A triumphant matador tosses his hat to the most beautiful woman in the arena who responds to a gallant victory by returning his hat.

QUEEN ELIZABETH WELCOMED IN NIGERIA

Her Majesty and the Duke of Edinburgh are greeted by the Governor General and other government officials.

A highlight of the welcoming ceremony is the presentation of a bouquet of flowers by a beautiful 4-year old child.

Nigerians dressed in their traditional costume await the arrival of Queen Elizabeth, the first reigning sovereign to visit the century-old West African crown colony.

Weddings

Some Talked-About Divorces

Ruth Roman & Mortimer W. Hall

Alfred Gwynne Vanderbilt & Jeanne Lourdes Murray Vanderbilt

Tyrus (Ty) Cobb & Frances Fairbairn Cass Cobb

Sonja Henie & William Gardiner

Elizabeth Taylor & Michael Wilding

Sammy Kaye & Ruth Kaye

Marie McDonald & Harry Karl

Edward G. Robinson & Mrs. Edward G. Robinson

Jeanne Crain & Paul Brinkman

Vivian Blaine & Manny G. Frank

Divorced Or Not Divorced – That Is The Question

JOHN JACOB ASTOR thought he had divorced his wife, Mrs. Gertrude Gretsch Astor in Mexico and proceeded to marry Dolores Fullman when lo and behold, the New York Supreme Court held the divorce invalid and granted a separation instead. In the meantime, John separated from Dolores which translates into being separated from not one but two wives. Keep that checkbook handy, John.

Marilyn Monroe & Playwright Arthur Miller In London.

Leslie Caron & Peter Hall

Willie Mays & Marghuerite Wendelle

Terry Moore & Eugene McGrath

Polly Bergen & Freddie Fields

Aldous Huxley & Laura Achera

Julius La Rosa & Rosemary Meyer

Audrey Meadows & Randolph Rouse

Dave Garroway & Pamela Wilde Kastner de Coninck

Shirley Jones & Jack Cassidy

Carol Channing & Charles Franklin Lowe

Sharon Kay Ritchie & Don Cherry

Gregory Peck & Veronique Passani

Efrem Zimbalist Jr. & Loranda Stephanie Spalding

Treat yourself to beer

that stays *COOL*

93% longer

Look for the words:
**NO DEPOSIT
NO RETURN**

in <u>NEW</u> **QUART BOTTLES** *you don't return*

Let your own taste prove what scientists have confirmed in the laboratory.

Beer or ale in the new Party-Size Quart Bottle has it all over other nonreturnable containers . . . for cold-retention, for lip-smacking flavor. For instance, these big Party Quart Bottles keep your favorite brand *cool 93% longer* than 12-ounce cans. It's easy to make the test yourself.

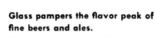

Glass pampers the flavor peak of fine beers and ales.

Prove this, too. Just let your favorite beer or ale aerate freely down the neck of the bottle, over the bottle's clean lip, straight into a glass. Let it form its natural head. The first refreshing sip tells you how important a bottle is to beer's protection . . . how important the neck of a bottle is to beer's flavor.

Pilsner illustrated is from Libbey's smartly styled Royal Fern line.

Party-Size Quart Bottles are the "life" of the party.

—5 glasses of your favorite beer at its best. If you are like most hosts, the big new Party-Size Quart Bottle will be your favorite for serving guests because it keeps beer within the just-right 40- to 50-degree temperature range far longer than when each guest has a separate small container.

Serve these PARTY-SIZE GLASS BOTTLES this weekend – *you <u>don't</u> have to take 'em back!*

NO DEPOSIT—NO RETURN BOTTLES
AN Ⓘ PRODUCT

Owens·Illinois
GENERAL OFFICES · TOLEDO 1. OHIO

72

What the Royals Do

ANTHONY EDEN and **CLEMENT ATTLEE** Become Knights Of The Order Of The Garter.

Duchess Of Windsor's Autobiography, *"The Heart Has Its Reasons"* Serialized In McCall's.

Happy Birthday, Queen Mum

Britain's Favorite Mum, Queen Mother Elizabeth Turns 56.

AGATHA CHRISTIE, MARGOT FONTEYN AND SIR OSBERT SITWELL Honored By Queen Elizabeth For Their Services To The Crown.

President Harry S. Truman Awarded Honorary Degree At Oxford.

President Truman's advice on the proper attire to wear for his daughter Margaret's upcoming wedding to dashing Clifton Daniel?

"The best pair of pants you've got, and just so long as you're covered up you'll be in style!"

TOASTING THE HOST THE MOST

In an impressive display of drinking prowess at a reception held at the Danish Embassy, Russia's Premier Nikolai Bulganin imbibed 20 martinis in an hour-and-a-half of toasting to a broad range of subjects.

Happy Birthday, Pope

1956 MARKS THE 17TH YEAR OF THE PONTIFF'S REIGN, A RELIGIOUS MILESTONE.

Catholics of the world rejoice on the 80th birthday of Pope Pius XII and the complete recovery of his health.

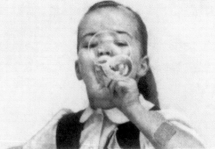
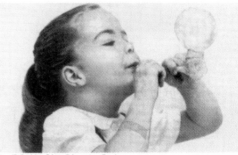

IRISH PRIME MINISTER VISITS WASHINGTON

John A. Costello, the first Prime Minister of Ireland ever to visit the United States, arrives in Washington for a state visit.

The Prime Minister receives a warm welcome from Vice President Richard Nixon and Undersecretary of State Herbert Hoover, Jr.

A hearty welcome from President Eisenhower, who will play host to Prime Minister Costello whose visit corresponds with St. Patrick's Day.

Roses For Miss Borchers

Actress Cornell Borchers arrives in the United States to receive recognition for her work in "Divided Heart."

The German actress makes her American debut this year with Rock Hudson in "Never Say Goodbye."

Broadway Stars Pay Tribute To Helen Hayes On The 50th Anniversary Of Her First Stage Appearance.

After A 16-Year Fight With Alcoholism, Lillian Roth Gets Rave Reviews For Her Performance At New York's Hotel Plaza.

GEORGE NADER
RECEIVES NAVY AWARD

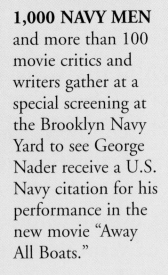

1,000 NAVY MEN and more than 100 movie critics and writers gather at a special screening at the Brooklyn Navy Yard to see George Nader receive a U.S. Navy citation for his performance in the new movie "Away All Boats."

Mamie Eisenhower Welcomes Mother of the Year

Mamie Eisenhower welcomes members of the Mother of the Year Committee.

The First Lady chats with honoree, Mrs. Jane Maxwell Pritchard, who was awarded the signal honor for 1956.

the most admired women

Eleanor Roosevelt
10th time in 11 years

Clare Boothe Luce

Mamie Eisenhower

Helen Keller

Queen Elizabeth II

Princess Margaret

Senator Margaret Chase Smith

Madame Chiang Kai-shek

Madame Vijaya Lakshmi Pandit

NEW *REO* MOWS ANY LAWN IN ONE CLEAN SWEEP

and you don't have to push!

Now you can give your entire lawn a neat, clipped, brushed look *with a mower that travels on its own power!*

The new Reo Power-Trim cuts grass beautifully, trims close, mulches leaves, chops weeds . . . and all *you* do is steer. It drives itself along at a normal walking speed. Takes grades in stride. Does the heavy work when you have to plow through high grass or weeds. Helps you finish faster— and fresher!

What's more, Reo's Front Wheel Drive gives you better *control* at all times. To turn or maneuver, just press down on the mower handle—driving wheels lift from ground. For really close trimming, just shift to neutral—mower becomes free-wheeling. Easy? Even the little woman can run it!

You can set blade at any of 4 cutting heights in seconds— without tools, without removing wheels. 21-inch model has an extra Creeper speed for heavy going in overgrown areas. Both models are powered by a rugged Reo 2¼ hp. 4-cycle easy-starting engine that runs on regular gas. Don't push a mower any more. Get behind a new Reo Power-Trim!

Exclusive Reo Design saves raking and sweeping. Reo Suction-Lift Blade is enclosed like a ducted fan. Strong suction pulls grass up for even cut, sprays the clippings out. Reo Triple Duty Door adjusts mower for any grass-cutting condition:

WIDE-OPEN for longest grass and weeds. Cuttings are shot out, away from mower. No clogging.

TOP OPEN for regularly mowed lawns. Clippings are spread out *evenly.* No windrows to rake.

CLOSED for fine-mulching of grass or leaves. Tiny mulched particles sift *into* lawn. No sweeping.

18-inch model, $149.95° **2-speed 21-inch model, $169.95°**
Other Reo Rotaries with same lawn-grooming features start at **$89.95°.** Write for name of your nearest Reo Dealer in the U. S. or Canada. °Slightly higher in West and Canada.

More than a million people mow with Reo

The greatest name in
POWER MOWERS
Sold and Serviced Everywhere

Product of Motor Wheel Corporation ● Lansing 3, Michigan, U.S.A.

COPYRIGHT 1956 BY MOTOR WHEEL CORP.

LITTLE NOTHINGS

* **JAYNE MANSFIELD** *(right)* **Named Miss Negligee Of 1956 By Underwear-Negligee Associates Convention In Manhattan.**

* **Roving U. P. Columnist Gloria Swanson Congratulates GRACE KELLY On Making The Flat-Chested Look Both Fashionable And Desirable.**

* **ANITA EKBERG, Sweden's Sultry Actress, Loses The Upper Portion Of Her Skin-Tight Strapless Gown In Posh London Hotel. Major Fallout!**

IT'S ENOUGH
TO MAKE YOU SIT DOWN AND CRY

Johnnie Ray Almost Loses His Shirt As Adoring Teen-Age Fans Rip His Clothes After Breaking Through Barricades In Sydney, Australia.

A BLUSHING MARLON BRANDO

Is Left Stammering As 100 Filipino Bobby-Soxers With Raging Hormones Crash His News Conference To Get A Look At The American Movie Star.

ED SULLIVAN SUFFERS INJURIES IN HEAD-ON CAR CRASH.

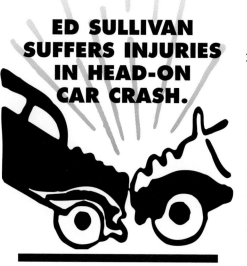

Dean Martin & Jerry Lewis
End Their 10-Year Partnership.

DAILY NEWS

Kirk Douglas sues Walt Disney

Actor Kirk Douglas Sues Walt Disney And ABC For Invasion Of Privacy, Charging Home Movies Shot In Disney's Home During A Social Visit Were Shown On Television Without His Consent.

Costello

◆ Frank Costello Begins 5-Year Jail Sentence For Income Tax Evasion.

◆ Labor Racketeer Johnny Dioguardia Arrested Along With Four Others In Acid-Throwing Attack Blinding Of Columnist Victor Riesel.

◆ Tokyo Rose Is Released From Prison After Serving Her Sentence For Committing Treasonable Acts During World War II.

◆ Playwright Clifford Odets Jailed For Drunken Driving After Leaving Scene Of Accident.

◆ Mail-Order Heir Montgomery Ward Thorne Is Found Dead In Chicago Slum After Apparent Sex-And-Drug Orgy.

◆ The Great John Barrymore's Daughter, Diana, Checks Into A Sanitarium For Her Drinking Problem.

HOWARD HUGHES Receives Eviction Notice From The City Of Long Beach, California To Remove His Experimental Flying Boat, The Hercules, Which Has Been In Storage Since 1947.

FBI Director, **J. EDGAR HOOVER,** Declares The Word "Cop" Unfavorable, Requesting Use Of A More Respectful Term – Police Officer.

Oral Roberts Asked To Leave ?

Defending accusations by a group of Australian preachers who called him a fraud and an imposter and insisted that he leave the country immediately, the flamboyant and prosperous Rev. Oral Roberts insisted that he was a child of God and that Christ had no objections to prosperity.

EVERYTHING YOU EVER NEEDED TO KNOW ... AT SIDWELL FRIENDS SCHOOL

Stunned by announcement by their children's school, Washington's Sidwell Friends School, that they would be admitting a number of qualified black students to their kindergarten class, avid segregationists Senator and Mrs. James O. Eastland consoled themselves by the fact that since their children had already completed kindergarten, it was unlikely that they would have any black classmates.

ROMANO MUSSOLINI, Il Duce's Youngest Son, Makes His Jazz Piano Debut At San Remo's International Jazz Festival.

WHITE DOVE SOUP
Cures Madame Chiang Kai-shek's Skin Rash.

A HOT TIME IN THE OLD HOUSE TONIGHT

Sir Winston Churchill awoke after a good night's sleep to learn that he had slept right through a small fire that erupted in his kitchen just a few steps away from his bedroom.

Presidential Candidate Senator Estes Kefauver Receives Endorsement From Head Of The Brotherhood Of Sleeping Car Porters Stating Kefauver's Favorable Civil Rights Position.

Jackie Robinson Receives NAACP's Spingarn Medal For Highest Achievement By An African-American.

President Eisenhower Appoints William Joseph Brennan, Jr. Associate Justice Of The U.S. Supreme Court.

Plenty of zoom at the top

IT HAPPENS right at the top of gas pedal travel.

Your foot goes down—maybe less than an inch—and Dynaflow Drive* comes up with a spang-new getaway that opens your eyes.

Suppose, for example, you want to enter the stream of traffic—or change your lane—or alter course.

Whatever you want to do, a bare touch of your toe achieves it. With sure confidence. With greater safety than ever before.

And light-footing the treadle like this, you save a pretty penny on gasoline in the bargain.

But that's not the whole of it. Not by a long shot!

For there's still *another*, still a *greater* take-off waiting for your call. It's the full-power switch-pitch breakaway you get by pressing the pedal all the way down.

It's like the giant hand of a friendly genie whisking you out of trouble. And brother, it's a boon just knowing it's there.

This is truly something you deserve to enjoy . . .

The thrill of command behind a big 322-cubic-inch Buick V8 engine—so brimful of live power that at 50 m.p.h., nine-tenths of its potential remains in reserve . . .

The feel of a lithe-handling, lighthearted and luxurious Buick—a suavely styled and beautifully engineered Buick—a 1956 Buick that's the blue-ribbon best of a true-blooded breed.

Actually, it's almost easier done than said. We have a demonstration car on the ready line if you have a few minutes to match it.

So why hold back? Drop in this week and start things moving!

*New Advanced Variable Pitch Dynaflow is the only Dynaflow Buick builds today. It is standard on Roadmaster, Super and Century—optional at modest extra cost on the Special.
†Standard on Roadmaster and Super, optional at extra cost on other Series.

NEW Precision-Balanced Chassis, engineered all new from front to rear for extra-rugged roadability

NEW V8 Power Peaks in Every Buick

NEW Variable Pitch Dynaflow*— with double-action take-off

NEW Deep-Oil-Cushioned Luxury Ride—with all-coil springing and true torque-tube drive

NEW Sweep-Ahead Styling— with Fashion Color Harmony inside and out

NEW Smoother-Action Brakes with Suspended Pedal

NEW Stepped-up Gas Mileage in All Buicks

NEW Safety Power Steering†— for instant and constant response

—and 97 Other New Features

SEE JACKIE GLEASON ON TV— Every Saturday Evening

When better automobiles are built Buick will build them

See Your Buick Dealer

Human Interest

1956 *is a* LEAP *year*

On the Chinese calendar, 1956 is the *Year of the Monkey*. According to Chinese folklore, those born in the year of the monkey are fun, loving, cheerful, energetic, clever, charming, talented and friendly. They can also be deceptive and unreasonable. Famous folks who fall under the sign of the monkey include: **Julius Caesar, Leonardo da Vinci, Alexander Dumas** and **Elizabeth Taylor**.

JUST THE FACTS

President
DWIGHT D. EISENHOWER
Vice President
RICHARD M. NIXON

World Population
2,834,158,518

The **U.S. Army** gets it's first official flag, designed by the Quartermaster Corps.

UNITED STATES ARMY
1775

HOSPITAL MOVE:
TRUCKS TRANSFER 300 PATIENTS IN TWO HOURS

In Evansville, Indiana, Operation Good Neighbor aids in the evacuation of St. Mary's Hospital with 110 pieces of rolling stock taking part in the transfer of the patients, beds and all.

One hour and forty minutes later the first batch of 90 patients are safely in the new hospital.

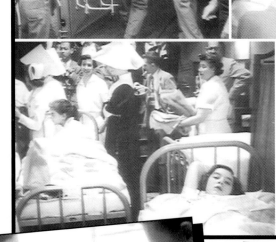

Patients are carefully loaded into tractor vans attended by nuns and nurses for the 7-mile trip to the new building.

Harvard To Raise Tuition $200, Increasing The College Cost To $1,000 And $1,200 For The Business School.

The First Climate-Controlled Shopping Center Opens Outside Of Minneapolis, Attracting Over 40,000 Potential Customers.

Perry H. Young Becomes The First Black Crew Member On An American Airline On Being Hired By A Helicopter Company, New York Airways.

Margaret E. Towner Becomes The First Woman To Be Ordained As A Minister By The Presbyterian Church In Syracuse, New York.

"Dear Abby" Makes Its Debut For The McNaught Syndicate.

New York Coliseum Opens.

U.S. Postal Service Issues First Stamp Designed To Emphasize Importance Of Wildlife Conservation.

Columbus, Ohio Zoo Reports First Gorilla Born In Captivity.

YOU WANT ME TO SAY HOW MANY HAIL MARYS??

Angered by his priest, and guided by an inner voice, a young Englishman throws open the door of his confessional and punches the priest in the eye.

A BOX OFFICE FLOP

A Los Angeles thief with a flair for the dramatic walks up to a movie box office, whips out a gun and demands everyone's money back on the grounds that he didn't like the film.

MANEUVERS AT 40 BELOW ZERO

NORTH POLE 802 MILES

FORT BRAGG, N.C. HOME OF 82ND AIRBORNE 3500 MILES

The 82nd Airborne makes their jump, landing on a frozen fjord with a layer of ice 55 inches thick.

Burdened by parachutes and bulky parkas, 700 paratroopers board their planes in Greenland for Exercise Arctic Night.

The paratroopers dig snow shelters to keep warm.

The biggest dry land regatta in history is launched as the National Motorboat Show opens in New York.

With an increasing number of Americans involved in boating, outboard motors attract a great deal of attention.

The show features every nautical need from this $11,000 outboard beauty to a $50 home assembly pram to a luxury cruiser priced in excess of $100,000.

876 TWO-DOOR CATALINA

860 TWO-DOOR CATALINA

STAR CHIEF TWO-DOOR CATALINA

Pontiac Covers The Fiel

Meet America's "first family" of hardtops—six gorgeous two- a
four-door models, Catalina styled as only Pontiac can do it.

What a field to choose from: three price ranges, two whe
bases, two horsepower options and so wide a variety of col
and fabrics that virtually the only limit on your choice is y
own imagination!

Here are cars that beg for action in every long, sleek, lux
ous line! When you give them the nod to go—they go—like
car has ever gone before! You feel the instant surge of 227 h

THE CAR SAYS "GO" AND THE PRICE WON'T STOP YOU!

870 FOUR-DOOR CATALINA

860 FOUR-DOOR CATALINA

STAR CHIEF FOUR-DOOR CATALINA

With Hardtops

g horsepower smoothed almost beyond belief by Pontiac's
clusive Strato-Flight Hydra-Matic*.

While you're thrilling to the greatest "go" on wheels, you're
laxing in the solid comfort of Pontiac's spacious interiors, extra-
g wheelbase and cradled ride. You enjoy, too, the safety of
ontiac's rugged construction and easy handling.

So when you're caught by the hardtop mood—and it likely
ill be soon—pay us a visit. You'll find exactly the car you
ant—at exactly the price you want to pay.   *An extra cost option.

'56 STRATO-STREAK

PONTIAC

SEE YOUR PONTIAC DEALER

89

NEW SUBWAY IN LENINGRAD

Russia's second-largest city opens a new subway system with tunnels that fan out from the city center to serve outlying industrial areas.

TOP: The opening is marked by ranking dignitaries from Moscow.

ABOVE: The first train leaves the central station with a group of factory workers.

LEFT: Scenes of Russian history are depicted in the ornate stations.

FEDERATION OF JEWISH PHILANTHROPIES PRESENTS AWARDS

Dinner guests gather at the Hotel Sheraton Astor for the third annual presentation of achievement awards by the Amusement Division of the Federation of Jewish Philanthropies.

While honorees **Kim Novak** and **Phil Silvers** kibitz with each other after receiving their awards; Steve Allen, star of "The Benny Goodman Story," presents an award to **Paul Muni**.

SOME TOP MAGAZINES

Saturday Evening Post

Collier's

LIFE

Better Homes and Gardens

LOOK

Readers' Digest

Family Affairs

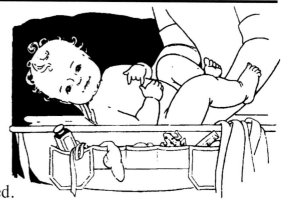

A recent study conducted by a domestic relations expert reveals that while children can sometimes hold a marriage together, they can also contribute to its break-up, while another study shows that children of broken marriages were better adjusted than children of parents who were unhappily married.

❖ **Couples In Their Fifties Become Closer To Their Spouses And Get New Enjoyment Out Of Life After Their Children Leave Home.**

❖ **Resolution Opposing Interfaith Marriages As A Threat To The Faith Of The Catholic Spouse And Religious Training Of The Children Is Adopted By The National Catholic Family Life Convention.**

○ A Cleveland Woman Sues Her House Painter After He Painted Her Arm Red When She Criticized The Quality Of His Work.

○ Women In Their Thirties Return To The Workforce, Finding Even The Most Menial Jobs More Stimulating Than Staying At Home.

○ Women With Higher Education Have Fewer Children Than Their Less Educated Counterparts.

○ Under A New Social Security Amendment, Women Would Become Eligible For Benefits At 62 Instead Of 65.

MARRIED MEN GET POOR PRESS IN THE COMICS

A New York University professor made the following observation with respect to how married men are depicted in comic strips:

☞ His wife's scapegoat   ☞ His children's dupe

☞ His children's dupe   ☞ Wishy-washy bungler

☞ Undependable in times of crisis

☞ Continually frustrated

☞ Generally inferior to his wife

Single men, on the other hand, are shown to be extremely masculine and dominate beautiful, but dependent, women.

Milwaukee Housewife Sues Her Husband For Divorce On The Grounds He Keeps Singing The Same Song Over And Over —

"I Wish I Were Single Again".

On being a female teenager...

the most commonly asked questions

- Should you kiss a boy on the first date?
- Is it healthy to go steady?
- How can I get that special someone interested in me?
- How can I overcome my shyness and not be a wallflower?
- How do I cope with other women in his life?
- How can I become better friends with my parents?
- What can I do about my differences with my parents on how to dress?
- How can I get along better with my younger siblings?
- Is the popular teen-ager happy and well adjusted?
- How do I make the right career choice?
- How do I introduce people properly and which fork should I use for each course?
- Should I go to college or get a job?
- If I plan to marry, is it worth the time and expense to get a college education?

THE COLLEGIATE WHEEL OF FORTUNE
THE EARNING STATISTICS

Average Tuition (Four Years): $9,000

Earnings Potential: $100,000 More Over A Lifetime Than A High School Graduate.

Exception: One-fourth of college graduates will earn less than the average holder of a high school diploma only.

Psycho Babble

Here's Looking At You, Kid or The Look Of.... Is In Your Eyes

A New York psychiatrist explored the hidden meaning behind a variety of looks and came to the following conclusions:

KIND OF LOOK	MEANING
EXCESSIVE BLINKING	Reality Avoidance
FIXED, DEPRESSED GAZE	Need Of Consolation
DRAMATIC GAZE	Hides Inner Conflicts And Inferiority Complex
ABSENT GAZE	Defense Against People
AVERTED GAZE	Avoidance of Feelings And Responsibilities

More Psycho Babble

▌ Advertisers Who Hook Children To Their Products Between The Ages Of 7 To 18 Are Apt To Have Lifetime Loyalty.

▌ Bizarre Food Cravings Linked To Possible Physical Deficiencies.

▌ Contentment With Life And Acceptance Of Its Realities Decreases Boredom In Workplace.

▌ A Dramatic Increase In Navy Bad-Conduct Discharges Is Blamed On A Trend Toward Moral Decline And Irresponsibility Among Adolescents.

▌ Insisting That A Child Be Overly Concerned With Neatness Can Stifle Artistic Development.

▌ Unhappy Childhoods And Fear Of Failure Often Motivate Success Drive.

▌ Psychological Treatment Found More Effective In Treating Female Homosexuals Than Their Male Counterparts.

According To A Report Released By A Group Of New York Psychoanalysts, Homosexual Men Played With Dolls Instead Of Playing Baseball As Youngsters.

Pyromaniacs Found To Be Raised In Homes With Indifferent Mothers And Abusive Fathers And Set Fires In A Misguided Effort To Find Their Manhood.

YOUNGEST GOLFER TOURS COUNTRY TO RAISE FUNDS FOR THE BABE ZAHARIAS CANCER FUND

With the aplomb of a grown-up and the polish of a pro, 5-year old golf child prodigy, Linda Lewis, swings away at the Clearview Course on Long Island.

Mildred "Babe" Didrikson Zaharias was an American athlete who excelled in golf and athletics. An Olympic Gold Medal winner and a record-shattering pro golfer, Zaharias died from cancer in 1956 while still in golfing's top ranks.

Linda's dad demonstrates his utmost confidence and lets her really get his teeth into one of her shots.

President Of Nichols Wire & Aluminum Co. Believes A Low-Cost Disposable Car Will Dominate The American Auto Market By 1966.

- Suburban Housing Boom Sweeps America.

- 840,000 Students Deprived Of Full-Time Classroom Instruction Due To Teacher Classroom Shortage.

- GasolineRationing Returns To Great Britain.

- U.S. Consumption Of Newsprint Reaches All-Time High Despite Severe Paper Shortage.

- Post-War Airplane Passenger Travel Increases Dramatically, Matching Number Of Train Passengers.

- Aviation Safety Record Set For Domestic Commercial Airlines.

  - U.S. Navy Icebreaker Reports Antarctic Iceberg Twice The Size Of Connecticut.

    - Swiss Expedition Scales Mt. Everest And Is The First To Climb Lhotse.

    - Kashmir's Mt. Gasherbrum, Second Highest Unclimbed Mountain, Scaled By Austrian Team Led By Fritz Moravec.

$10,000 A YEAR LIFESTYLE

- Upper Stratum Of Community
- Good Schools For Children
- Comfortable House
- Nice Car
- Good Credit

DAILY COST OF TRAVELLING TO WORK

By Car . . . . $.26

Bus Or Subway . . . . $.28

The Annual Earning Potential Of Those Born In 1956 Is Expected To Be Around $8,000 By The Year 2000.

Here's The Dope On Dope

➠ The U.S. has more drug addicts than all other Western nations combined.

➠ Illegal drug traffic has tripled since World War II.

➠ Drug addicts commit an estimated 50% of urban crimes.

In A 5-To-4 Decision, The U.S. Supreme Court Holds That New York City Did Not Have The Right To Dismiss A Professor For Invoking The Protection Of The 5th Amendment.

IRS Shuts Down Left-Wing Publication, DAILY WORKER, For Tax Evasion.

PRESIDENT EISENHOWER

■ **Approves Bill Authorizing Death Penalty For Selling Or Giving Heroin To Anyone Under 18**

■ **Signs Historic Public Works Bill Authorizing Over $33 Billion For Nationwide Network Of Highways Linking Major American Cities**

■ **Authorizes FBI Intervention In Kidnapping Cases 24 Hours After Commission Of The Crime Instead Of The Former 7-Day Waiting Period**

■ **Creates Federal Council On Aging**

Crest Toothpaste Is Distributed Nationally.

THE FBI SOLVES THE BRINK'S ROBBERY AFTER A 5-YEAR INVESTIGATION... **NO MONEY IS TRACED OR RECOVERED.**

Pepsodent Introduces Its Catchy Jingle:

"You'll Wonder Where The Yellow Went When You Brush Your Teeth With Pepsodent."

The Food & Drug Administration Rescinds Order Banning The Dying Of Oranges To Make Them Look More Appetizing.

Kentucky Fried Chicken Begins Franchising.

The "Trip Finder" A Group Of Sectional Highway Maps Is Introduced As A Travel Aid.

Among National Brands Adding Kosher Products To Their Lines:

Ⓚ **Beech-nut Heinz Brillo Curtiss Candy**

Col. Sanders

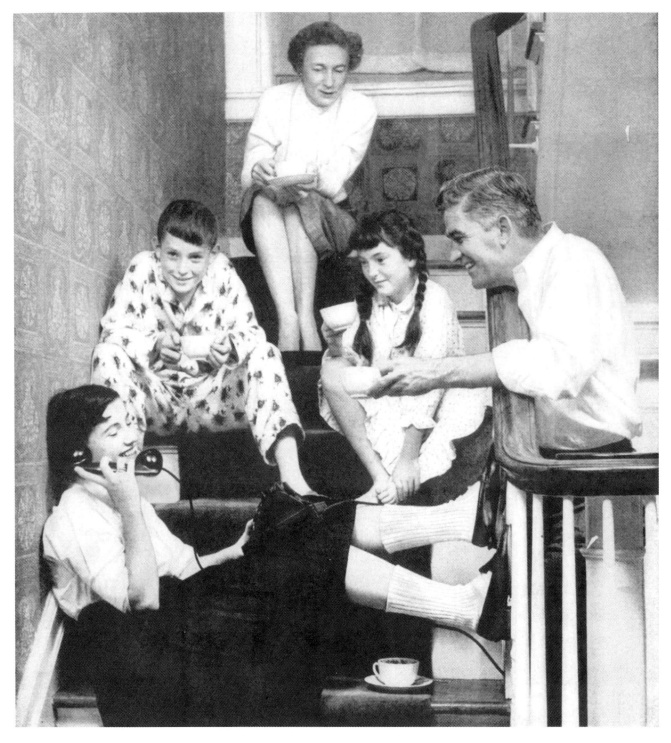

"He called her! Now we can go drink our Postum in peace!"

A phone call can be a very special thing . . . and you'll find Postum's unique flavor very *special*, too! Postum is *different* from everyday hot drinks . . . with a grain-rich, slow-roasted flavor you and your whole family will enjoy.

And Postum helps you top a satisfying day with a good night's sleep. It's 100% caffein-free . . . safe even for children! For less than a penny a cup— why not make this pleasant change from everyday hot drinks today?

*Enjoy the hot drink with a **different** flavor . . .*

A Product of
General Foods

New Words

ACCOMMODATION SALE
The sale of a commodity to another dealer for resale.

AFTERBURNER
A device for burning gas that passes through to the exhaust pipe of an automobile.

AWARDEE
To give (one) an award.

BARGANZA:

A bargain sale, or a group of bargains.

BRANE
Bombing Radar Navigation Equipment – an electronic device to direct an airplane to its target with great accuracy.

BRINKMANSHIP
The practice, especially in international politics, of seeking advantage by creating the impression that one is willing and able to pass the brink of nuclear war rather than concede.

EURATOM
European Atomic Pool.

CANYONEER
One who runs western rivers in various types of small boats.

FRONTAGE ROAD
On a limited access highway, a turnout road usually for a filling station or restaurant.

GREYLISTED
Partly, not completely, blacklisted.

MISSILRY
Guided missiles considered collectively.

MORTGAGE WAREHOUSING
The use of commercial bank credit on an interim basis by mortgage lenders.

MOTELERY
A huge, luxurious hotel designed for leisurely modern living, with some of the advantages of motels.

RAMPED STAGE
A stage sloping up at the rear to give better perspective.

ROLL ON, ROLL OFF
The system of shipping via water in which large loaded crates, trucks and railroad cars are rolled onto a ship at a port and rolled off at another.

ROLLOUT
The rolling of an airplane from a production line.

SEW-OFF
A final contest among home seamstresses.

SPLIT-TIME
A daylight saving time using a half hour rather than an hour advance.

STEEL BAND
A musical band, usually calypso, using oil drums.

STORM TRACKER
A device for gathering weather data.

TEAR-AWAY JERSEY
A football jersey that tears easily and cannot be used to keep a player from running when grasped by an opponent.

WINE-MOBILE
An automobile that dispenses wines.

ZIGZAG EATING:
Shifting one's fork to the other hand.

101

Hot-Rodders Turn Drag-Racing Into Sophisticated Sport

Motorized Go-Carts Debut In Los Angeles.

Navy Balloonists Soar To Record Altitude of 76,000 Ft.

USS SARATOGA, World's Biggest Warship, Is Commissioned At Brooklyn Navy Yard.

U.S. Air Force Chief Of Staff, **GENERAL NATHAN F. TWINING**, Authorized By Ike To Accept Invitation To Attend Soviet Air Show.

Snow Falls On Rivera As Severe Cold Wave Hits Europe.

U.S. Government Announces It Will Help Transport Over 1,000 Afghan Moslems On Their Pilgrimage To Mecca.

WHAT'S A FEW YEARS AMONG FRIENDS?

After medical authorities in New York examined Colombian Indian, Javier Pereira, who claimed to be 167 years old, they admitted that he might be more than 150 years old.

FOR A GUD TIEME, DOEN'T SPEL WEL

A study conducted at the University of California on the profile of a good speller revealed that women who are good spellers tend to be confident and possess social grace, while their male counterparts displayed the opposite qualities. It went on to say that the poor spellers from both sexes tended to be more relaxed about life in general, didn't need to be intellectual and were quite at ease in social situations.

Buddhism's 2,500 Anniversary Celebrated In India.

Trans-Atlantic Phone Service Begins, Linking Newfoundland to Scotland.

✎ 12-Year Old **FRED SAFIER, JR.** Is Awarded Harvard Scholarship After Making A Perfect Mark In Advanced Mathematics In His College Entrance Examination.

✎ **LEONARD ROSS**, A 10-Year Old Student From California, Wins $100,000 Prize On A TV Quiz Show For Answering Correctly Questions On The Stock Market.

The Short End Of The Chalk

Tokyo school officials defended their decision not to hire any teacher under 5 feet tall on the grounds that (**a**) it would be difficult to locate her during outdoor activities and (**b**) she would not be able to reach the blackboard.

AVOID OVERLOADING YOUR MEMORY

When You Go Grocery Shopping Memorize Only Seven Items To Buy, Which Is About The Number The Average Person Can Carry In His Mind At Any Single Time.

Nobel Peace Prize Committee Announces It Could Not Find A Worthy Recipient For The 1956 Prize

SOMETHING TO BARK ABOUT

The Westminster Kennel Club of New York took a historic step by awarding **Mrs. Bertha Smith**'s 6-lb. white toy poodle, Wilber White Swan, top honors. This was the first time a toy breed became champion.

Grey Squirrels Destroy Half-Million Dollars' Worth Of U.S. Telephone Cable Yearly — Bell Labs Suspend Costly Research, Stating Failure To Come Up With An Effective Deterrent.

Legendary Himalayan Abominable Snowman Footprints Spotted In French Alpine Resort Of Val-d'Isère.

- Ringling Bros. And Barnum And Bailey Circus Holds Its Last Performance Under A Tent, Opting To Switch To Large Indoor Venues.

- Philadelphia Court Engages In Unprecedented Experiment And Allows Press Photographer Inside Courtroom.

- Colorado Becomes First State To Allow Courtroom Coverage By Photographers, As Well As Radio And Television Reporters.

- The Automobile Ferry Ceases Operation In San Francisco Bay On Opening Of Richmond - San Rafael Bridge — The World's Second Longest High-Level Crossing.

• PASSINGS •

Jake "Greasy Thumb" Guzik,
Associate Of Al Capone, Dies At 69.

Samuel James Seymour,
Believed To Be Last Surviving Witness Of Lincoln's Assassination, Dies At 96.

Lewis Terman,
Creator Of The IQ Test, Dies At 79.

Albert Woolson,
Last Surviving Member Of The Civil War's Union Army, Dies In Duluth, Minnesota At 109.

Stop-Watch Tests Reveal That A Golfer Spends An Average 12 Minutes Of Actual Playing Time On An 18-Hole Course.

Armies Of Large **Red Ants** Attack Traffic Control Boxes In Los Angeles Causing Traffic Signal Failure.

103

"Mommy! Hurry home! Your new Norge Automatic's here... and sump'n you like came in it!"

TIDE'S INSIDE—NORGE KNOWS TIDE
GETS CLOTHES THE CLEANEST CLEAN POSSIBLE!

It stands to reason that the men who *make* the fine Norge Automatic are the men who really know all about it . . . know what's good for it . . . know how to make it give you the best possible results. And these men who make the Norge recommend *Tide* . . . actually put a box of Tide in every new machine right at the factory.

So *many* other manufacturers do the same. That's to make sure that right from the very first wash, their automatics work perfectly, give you the cleanest clothes possible.

In all these top-loading automatics, no leading washday product made, nothing else—with or without suds—can beat Tide for getting clothes clean.
Use Tide in *your* automatic and discover for yourself why more women use Tide in their automatics than any other washday product in America!

THE CLEANEST CLEAN POSSIBLE
IS TIDE-CLEAN

SEE THE NEW NORGE AUTOMATIC WASHER WITH EXCLUSIVE SUPER RINSE!

- Five totally different purifying actions flush away everything—from lint to sand, automatically!
- Exclusive Time-Line Control lets you select two separate automatic cycles— regular cycle for family loads—short cycle for small loads and delicate fabrics!

THE MAKERS OF 25 AUTOMATICS RECOMMEND *Tide!*

DISASTERS

Disasters of 1956

ANDREA DORIA SINKS
IN WATERS OFF NEW YORK

TWISTER DEVASTES
HUDSONVILLE, MICHIGAN

YUBA CITY, CALIFORNIA
THREATENED BY FLOOD

■ Collapse of shrine wall kills 125 during New Year's celebrations at Niigata, Japan.

■ Cold weather and storms result in $10 million damage to Florida crops.

■ Blizzard and intense cold wave in Western Europe kill 1,000 and cause crop damage estimated at $2 billion.

■ 162 deaths and $150 million property damage result from 4-day snowstorm in Northeastern U.S.

■ 30 are killed by bomb accidentally dropped from Thai Air Force plane.

■ Earthquake (7.7 on Richter scale) in northern Afghanistan kills 2,000.

■ Venezuelan Super-Constellation crashes in Atlantic off Asbury Park, NJ – all 74 aboard killed.

■ 208 firemen hurt during fire in abandoned Wanamaker's store in New York City.

■ 2,161 Chinese reported killed by floods caused by typhoon Wanda.

■ 262 killed in coal mine fire in Marcinelle, Belgium.

DISASTER AT SEA
ANDREA DORIA

The Italian luxury liner "ANDREA DORIA" sinks after a collision with Sweden's "Stockholm" in a crowded shipping lane near New York.

The "Ile de France", which headed the rescue work of 10 vessels, steams into New York with 700 survivors.

New York's piers are the scene of joyful reunions. Tragically, 50 had died but a major disaster was averted.

106

29 DIE, 142 HURT IN CALIFORNIA TRAIN WRECK

Hundreds of feet of track are ripped up as a Flyer overturns on a curve.

Most of the victims, predominantly servicemen on furlough, are pinned in the wreckage.

Investigators are on the scene immediately to try to determine the cause of this terrible disaster.

Disasters 1956

WORST AIR DISASTER IN COMMERCIAL AVIATION HISTORY OCCURS OVER THE GRAND CANYON AS TWO U.S. PLANES CARRYING 128 PEOPLE COLLIDE.

B-36 BOMBER CRASH

In a field near Denver, a B-36 bomber crashes and burns. It is a craft large enough to carry 21 crew members. Of the 21, two suffered injuries. The crash is blamed on power failer caused by ice in fuel lines.

President Eisenhower Announces Steps To Help Ease Acute Distress In U.S. Drought Areas.

Devastating Twisters Rip Through The Midwest

Hudsonville, Michigan is worst hit by a two-day series of storms that strike 14 states in the nation's midsection.

With 13 dead in Hudsonville, the rest of the residents escape with their lives and not much else.

Floods Threaten Yuba City

The Feather River menaces the levees guarding Yuba City, California.

Engineers closely watch the rising water and phone the alarm as the crest rises.

Weary residents prepare to evacuate for the third time in six weeks.

Residents trying to dry out from the previous flood, which cost 34 lives and $179 million, form a motorcade to take refuge on higher ground.

Eisenhower Declares California Major Disaster Area As A Result Of Devastating Flooding.

Nova Scotia
Crippled By Flood

A sudden thaw coupled with rain brings heavy flooding to Nova Scotia.

Near Halifax, hundreds of cars are lost as the water rises higher and higher.

Minor streams become raging torrents, sweeping away everything in their path.

Bridges are undermined and damage runs into the tens of millions.

WINTER STORM BATTERS CANARY ISLANDS

Torrential rains cause landslides destroying 57 homes and washing out bridges.

Winter Storm Strikes
Holland

Winter moves in on Holland with a raging snowstorm.

Amsterdam is particularly hard hit by the fall of 20 inches, which brings the railroad to a virtual standstill.

Spectators look at a car that skidded into one of the canals.

Her electronic assistant frees her to do far more valuable work

Open door to a glamour job

Voicewriter offers secretary bright, new horizons!

TODAY—there's a wonderful difference in Susan's life at the office. She's free to help her boss preview new fashions...greet clients...do a lot of preliminary "head work" for him. She has the passport to a more exciting job—the Edison Voicewriter.

For the streamlined Voicewriter on her desk frees her from hours of dull office routine. While her boss dictates, she's able to do the "extras"—become more of a real assistant.

Why don't you become one of the modern secretaries who have discovered how the Voicewriter gives you free time — more fun on the job. Your Edison Business Consultant will be glad to tell you about it. His telephone listing is Edison Voicewriter. Or write Thomas A. Edison, Incorporated, West Orange, N. J. for complete details.

The Voicewriter Secretarial—companion to the **Executive** Voicewriter—is your modern electronic assistant. Comes in 5 colors and can be personalized with golden initials. Why don't you find out how to put the Voicewriter on your team! The cost? As low as $15.00 a month!

Edison Voicewriter

Thomas A. Edison
INCORPORATED
PIONEER IN ELECTRONICS

What's New

What a kid dreams of.

New Products and Inventions

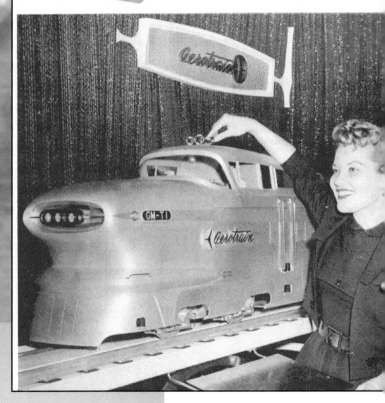

SELLING THE PRODUCTS YOU MAKE

GM's Motorama Explores the Future

The streamlined, air conditioned diesel *Aerotrain*, built by General Motors, carries 400 passengers. Using bus bodies on railroad wheels as coaches, it's low center of gravity promises fast, comfortable and less expensive rail travel.

Unfortunately, after being tested by three different railroads in actual passenger service, it is deemed a failure.

Singer Patty Page poses with a scale model of Aerotrain.

New Heat Protective Suit Passes Furnace Test

In New York, engineer D.J. Bennett prepares to enter an industrial furnace to demonstrate a new heat protecting fabric lighter and more flexible than a fireman's rubber slicker.

The fabric is a micro-thin layer of reflective aluminum bonded to a backing of asbestos or fiberglass and is unmatched in its resistance to intense radiant heat.

HE FLIES THROUGH THE AIR WITH THE GREATEST OF EASE

This combination helicopter and boat sails through the air, borrowing its get up and go from an outboard tow boat.

116

LARGEST TELESCOPE IN U.S. UNVEILED AT HARVARD.

BELL TELEPHONE
Begins "Visual Phone" Development.

Vending Machines
Offering Full-Course Hot Meals For $.75 Begin To Replace Factory Cafeterias.

Royal Typewriter
Introduces New Typewriter Ribbon In Two Plastic Containers Allowing User To Change Ribbons Without Soiling Her Hands.

MICROIMAGE Device Gives Automatic Access To Up To 10,000 Microfilm Frames.

Heated Flexible Windshield Glass To Protect Pilots From Collisions With Birds Is Developed By Pittsburgh Plate Glass Co.

Hughes Aircraft Company
Develops New Picture Tube With Stop-Action Capabilities For Air-Borne Radar.

Color Television Programs Can Now Be Recorded On Ampex Magnetic Tape With Up To 15 Minutes Of Programming For Rebroadcast.

Hand-Held TV Camera Developed For The U.S. Army.

JET PROPULSION ENGINES DEBUT AND GO INTO PRODUCTION.

"The Grasshopper"
is a robot weather station being tested at the Naval Research Laboratory for use in the Antarctic.

Looking more like a space creature, it stands up, raises its own antenna and other devices for weather recording.

The battery-powered robot transmits via radio data on wind speeds, temperature, pressure, etc., its signals being picked up 800 miles away.

MONSANTO CHEMISTRY IN ACTION . . . COMMUNICATIONS

BUSY AMERICANS ENJOY THE EXTRA STYLE, COMFORT AND CONVENIENCE THAT MONSANTO CHEMICALS ADD *(left to right)* TO TELEPHONES—GLARE-

MONSANTO TAPS CHEMISTRY TO

Mixing creative research with production know-how, Monsanto tailors myriads of

NEW HEARING AID HIDES behind your ear, takes up only one cubic inch of space, operates with a flick of your finger. The tiny transmitter—including case made of Monsanto plastic—weighs less than an ounce. In a few minutes, you forget you have it on! Simple one-piece construction makes sound reception more natural than ever before, eliminates cords and bulky attachments.

DON'T BLAME YOUR PEN! Fuzzy writing (above, left) is no problem with stationery that has been treated with Monsanto chemicals. This fine paper (right) takes *and holds* a sharp ink line. Other Monsanto products lower the cost of making paper, help produce clearer blueprints . . . brighter paper . . . blacker inks with more body. Monsanto chemicals also help to mask printing ink odor.

REDUCING TV PICTURE FRAMES AND GLASS—LIGHT, COLORFUL RADIO CABINETS—UNBREAKABLE RECORDS—EASY-TO-READ BOOKS AND NEWSPAPERS

SERVE A LOOKING, LISTENING U. S.

products to meet the needs of people. Here are a few examples in Communications

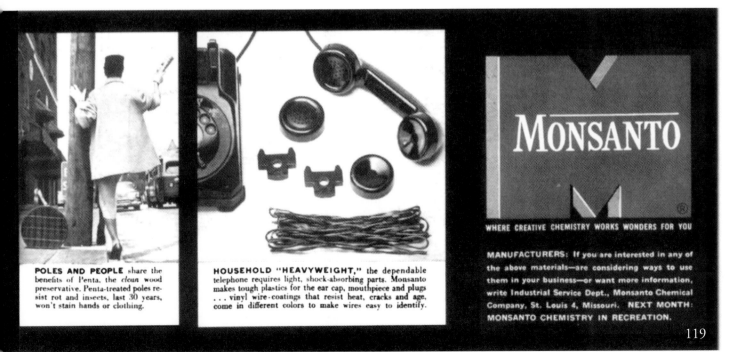

ZENITH RADIO CORP. Introduces "Space Command TV"– A Remote Tuner That Controls The TV Set.

 GENERAL ELECTRIC And THE WESTINGHOUSE ELECTRIC CORP. Introduce Colored Light Bulbs For The Home.

Tiny Home Fire Alarm Developed By Laramie Chemical Corp. Of Stamford, Connecticut.

BRITISH INVENTOR DEVELOPS FIRST SOLAR ENERGY HOUSE.

Central Air Conditioning System Introduced By
AMANA REFRIGERATION, INC.

ELECTRONIC DEVICES OF THE FUTURE

• Equipment to heat or cool a room silently by electronic panels.

• A magnetic tape player that reproduces television programs using standard television receivers.

• An electronic light amplifier that increases up to 1,000 times the brightness of a projected image, including X-ray images of stationary objects.

☐ Kodak Introduces Kodacolor Film Which Enables The Photographer To Use The Same Film For Indoor Or Outdoor Shots.

☐ Bell & Howell Introduces Automatic Movie Camera Which Sets The Lens At The Proper Exposure.

☐ General Motors Introduces Ultrasonic Dishwasher Which Uses Sound Waves To Remove Dirt As Part Of Its "Kitchen Of Tomorrow."

☐ Leroy Crozier Of Cincinnati, Ohio Invents A Portable Ironing Board.

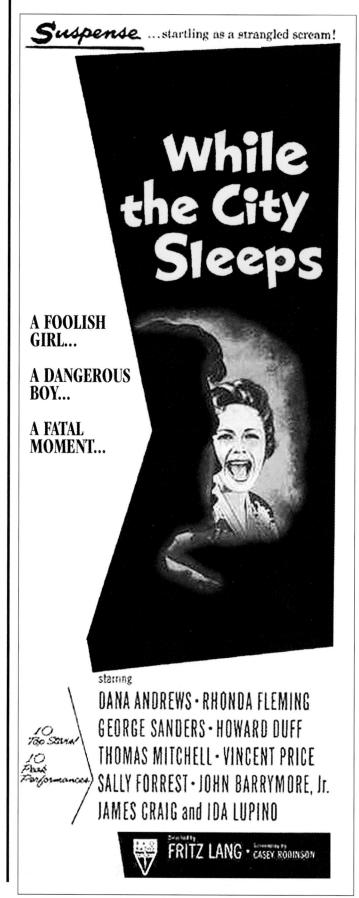

FLUORIDE TOOTHPASTE

Produces A 42% Reduction In Tooth Decay When Tested On 300 College Freshmen.

Long-life Stainless Steel Razor Blades Introduced By British Company, Wilkinson Sword.

Aerosol Spray-On Shoe Polish Developed By Power-Matic Corp.

"Instantizing" New Process Is Developed For Mixing Dried Foods.

Aerosol Containers Revolutionize The Cosmetic Industry.

RUBBER SCRUBBER CROP.

Of Watertown, New York, Invents New Household Scouring Device With Foam Rubber On One Side And An Abrasive Material On The Other.

LIQUEFIED GAS PRODUCED ON AN INDUSTRIAL SCALE

Johnson & Johnson

Introduces A Non-Slip Cotton-Gauze Roller Bandage.

NEW CAR SAFETY DEVICES

▶ Latches that reduce the likelihood of doors flying open in crashes;

▶ Padding on instrument panels and visors;

Seat belts!

PASSINGS

Cesare Barbieri,

Inventor Of Auto Antifreeze And Machines To Make Paper Cups, Dies At 78.

" THANK YOU THESE STAMPS ARE SANITARY "

The U.S. Post Office has introduced **"The Stampmaster,"** an automatic stamp dispenser which not only makeschange and deliversstamps, but even has a built-in speaker to thank the customer and reassure her thatthe stamps are sanitary as well as a reminder to think about buying more now to save another trip to the post office.

GIANT FORGING PRESS

Largest Machine In The World, Goes Into Full Operation In North Grafton, Massachusetts.

NEW Packaging And Scanning Machinery Moves Production Line Of Consumer Goods Faster And Diminishes Mislabelling Possibilities.

The Mechanics And Farmers Savings Bank in Bridgeport, Connecticut, Introduces A Two-Way Screen And Speaker Set-Up Allowing The Customer To Communicate With The Teller Without Ever Leaving His Car.

This Christmas...

Give the most gifted portable

...with the ribbon you never touch

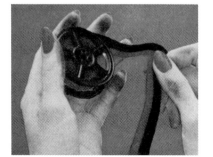

No more smudgy fingers with Royal's new TWIN-PAK, the quick change ribbon. Your hands never touch the ribbon.

To Change the ribbon on the new 1957 Royal Portable, just lift out the old TWIN-PAK...drop in the new. There's nothing to wind! Nothing to thread! It's as quick, clean and simple as this.

FOR STUDENTS and grownups alike, there's no Christmas gift that gives more than a new Royal Portable. It takes the "dirty work" out of writing. Helps to raise marks. Improves spelling. Teaches neatness and accuracy.

And the new Royal Quiet Deluxe® is the "most gifted" portable of all time...with the new Royal TWIN-PAK: the quick change ribbon that makes messy old ribbon changing a "cinch."

And that's only the beginning! There's the extra ruggedness of a Royal...the Magic® Margin...the "light-as-air" touch ...and the two extra keys!

Strikingly handsome, the new Royal comes in six exciting colors. Equipped with standard-size keyboard and controls. It's by far the biggest Christmas gift value we've ever offered.

Why not make this a Royal Christmas? There's no down payment required, and up to 24 months to pay at most Royal Portable dealers'. See *your* Royal dealer today!

1957 **ROYAL**® Portables with TWIN-PAK...the <u>only</u> Quick Change Ribbon!

Royal Typewriter Company, *Division of Royal McBee Corporation*

122

Science

Scientists Report Surface Of Venus Too Hot To Support Life As We Know It.

Cosmic Rays Bombard Earth At Phenomenal Rate Indicating Cosmic Rays Can Originate In The Solar System As Well As Outer Space.

Earth's First Man-Made Satellite Nears End Of Planning Stage.

THE ARMY MAP SERVICE REPORTS EARTH 420 FEET SMALLER THAN HAS BEEN THOUGHT.

Nobel Prize Winning Scientist **Sir George Thomson** Of Cambridge, England Predicts Monkeys Will Be Trained To Perform Certain Types Of Routine Work.

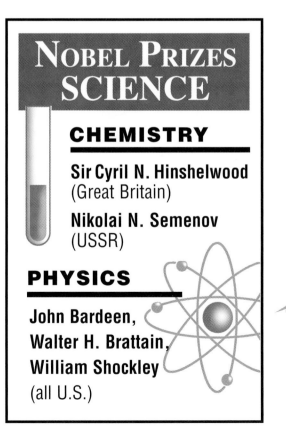

NOBEL PRIZES SCIENCE

CHEMISTRY

Sir Cyril N. Hinshelwood
(Great Britain)

Nikolai N. Semenov
(USSR)

PHYSICS

John Bardeen,
Walter H. Brattain,
William Shockley
(all U.S.)

ATOMIC EXPERT WARNS THAT MAJOR TECHNICAL OBSTACLES MUST BE OVERCOME IN ORDER TO DEVELOP PRACTICAL, LOW-COST NUCLEAR POWER.

SCIENTISTS PREDICT GLOBAL WARMING TREND FOR THE NEXT 100 YEARS.

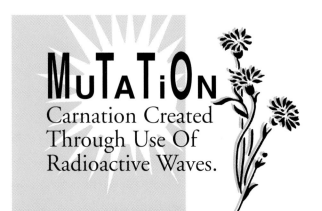

MuTaTiOn
Carnation Created Through Use Of Radioactive Waves.

Israeli Scientists Develop Test To Determine Sex Of Fetus After Twelfth Week Of Pregnancy By Extracting Sample Of Amniotic Fluid.

DR. LANDRUM B. SHETTLES Of Columbia University Develops Procedure For Determining The Sex Of An Unborn Baby Through Amniotic Fluid Extracted In The Ninth Month Of Pregnancy. Technique For Safe Extraction Still Being Worked On.

University of California Announces The Discovery Of The Antineutron, A New And Previously Unknown Particle, With The Property Of Destroying Matter In Its Ordinary State.

- ✴ The Neutrino, Atomic Particle With No Electric Charge, Discovered At Los Alamos Laboratory In U.S.

- ✴ Ion Microscope Developed by F.W. Muller.

- ✴ Nuclear Reactor Opens In Harwell, England.

- ✴ AEC Approves Private Nuclear Reactor In Indian Point, N.Y.

Radiation Victims Who Do Not Vomit Immediately After Exposure Have Higher Rate Of Survival Than Those Who Vomit Immediately After Being Exposed.

PASSINGS

Dr. Hans S. Joachim, Ex-Aide To Einstein, Developer Of Sound-Guided Torpedo, Dies At 68.

AEROCYCLE

The U.S. Army Buys Experimental Models Of An Aerocycle, A One-Man Flying Machine Designed To Give The Infantryman More Mobility.

First Films Of Ground-To-Air Guided Missiles In Action Released By Great Britain.

What do you mean, it won't fly?

An Australian astronomer **Richard van der Riet Woolley** shook up the world of space research, declaring that no one will ever put up enough money to fund space travel. Leonard Carter of the British Interplanetary Society promptly declared that the first flight to the moon will take place in the next twenty years. Indignant Interplanetary Society Council member Kenneth Gatland added his opinion that space travel is inevitable and that toward the end of the century manned vehicles will orbit the moon with actual landings.

New wonder of nutrition found in the fresh orange

The BIO-FLAVONOIDS, mysterious yellow substances in the "meat" of the fruit, affect your family's health in a special way all their own

The list of health values in the fresh orange has continued to mount through the years... vitamin C, pro-vitamin A, B vitamins, minerals, amino acids, the remarkable protopectins.

Now the bio-flavonoids are making front-page news. Science knows now that the bio-flavonoids, when teamed with vitamin C in oranges, fortify body health from childhood to old age in a new way largely overlooked in the past.

They have a direct effect on the capillary system ... the millions of tiny blood vessels that nourish every part of your body. They help keep these tiny vessels strong and elastic ... efficient in their job. They also strengthen weak capillaries. Thus, when combined with other factors in the fresh orange, they have an important bearing on the prevention of disease, the way your children grow, the way you look and feel!

One Sunkist Orange a day gives you a rich supply of bio-flavonoids. They are abundant in the fresh orange but not in processed juice. Like the recently announced protopectins, they are found almost entirely in the "meat" of the fresh orange. And they are scarce in most other foods.

Shouldn't you see that each member of your family eats one fresh orange every day?

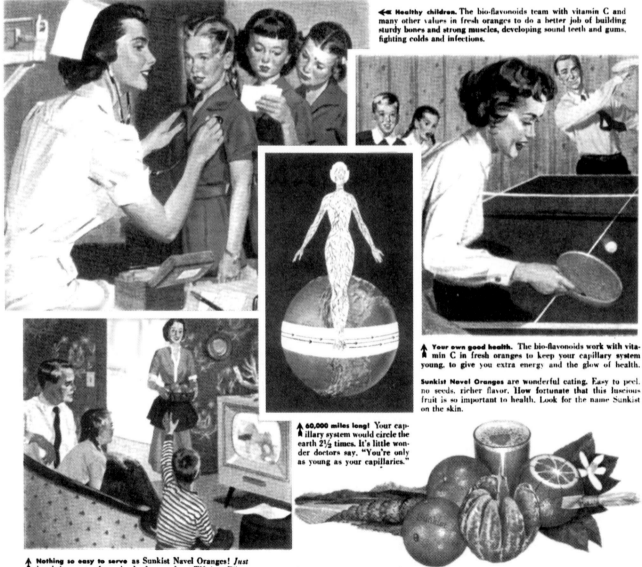

◄◄ **Healthy children.** The bio-flavonoids team with vitamin C and many other values in fresh oranges to do a better job of building sturdy bones and strong muscles, developing sound teeth and gums, fighting colds and infections.

▲ **Your own good health.** The bio-flavonoids work with vitamin C in fresh oranges to keep your capillary system young, to give you extra energy and the glow of health.

Sunkist Navel Oranges are wonderful eating. Easy to peel, no seeds, richer flavor. How fortunate that this luscious fruit is so important to health. Look for the name Sunkist on the skin.

▲ **60,000 miles long!** Your capillary system would circle the earth 2½ times. It's little wonder doctors say, "You're only as young as your capillaries."

▲ **Nothing so easy to serve** as Sunkist Navel Oranges! *Just hand them out*—after school, after meals, at TV time. When you squeeze them for juice, don't strain it. Keep the healthful solids that contain the bio-flavonoids and so many other values.

Sunkist Growers *California-Arizona Navel Oranges*

Eat whole fresh oranges—drink whole fresh orange juice!

Medicine

POLIO

SALK POLIO VACCINE
Made Available To Public –
JONAS SALK Predicts
Elimination Of Polio By 1959.

*New Findings Suggest
That Booster Polio Shots
May Not Be Necessary
After Initial Immunization
By Salk Vaccine.*

*DR. ALBERT SABIN
Develops Oral Polio Vaccine.*

NOBEL PRIZES MEDICINE

Andre F. Cournand
(U.S.)

Werner Forssman
(Germany)

Dickinson W. Richards, Jr.
(U.S.)

THE YEAR OF BIRTH CONTROL

Women Test First Birth
Control Pill In Puerto
Rico And Haiti.

**According To Dr. Nathan
Millman Of The Ortho
Research Foundation
In New Jersey, There Is
No Magic Birth Control
Tablet That Can Produce
Temporary Sterility
In A Patient.**

Successful Pregnancy Rate
Low For Women 44 Years
Of Age Or Older According
To Report Released By
Dr. E.F. Stanton.

**A post-war orthopedic
disorder has developed
in Great Britain called
"espresso wrist" as a result
of twisting the hand during
the preparation of demi-
tasse. The cure: hold the
wrist straight.**

A WONDERFUL NEW WAY TO CONTROL WEIGHT

NEW Pearson sakrin

The ONLY Liquid Sweetener with DARAMIN®, containing
NO Calories! NO Sugar! NO Salt!

Use it in coffee, tea, hot or cold beverages, mixed drinks, cereals, desserts, cooking!

It's *super-concentrated*—only 1 drop equals the sweetness of 1 whole teaspoon of sugar!

NEW PEARSON LIQUID SAKRIN PUTS SWEETNESS IN, LEAVES CALORIES OUT—will help you be slim, stay slim, look better, feel better—every meal, every day. And you'll sacrifice *nothing* in flavor or enjoyment!

Excess weight is a threat to your health. Science shows that heart disease, high blood pressure and many other ills are more common in overweight persons. *Only 100 calories extra a day can put on ten extra pounds of fat a year!* PEARSON SAKRIN can help you avoid *hundreds* of extra calories a day.

1 DROP equals 1 TSP. SUGAR

EACH DROP SAVES CALORIES!

One tiny drop of PEARSON SAKRIN from its attractive squeezable dropper bottle—gives you the sweetening power of 1 teaspoon of sugar *without any of its calories!* In just coffee, tea, with desserts and in cooking, it can save you up to 511 calories and more a day—that equals over one pound of weight a week in "sweetening calories" alone!

Unlike some sweeteners that require you to use 2 to 5 drops per teaspoon of sugar, just 1 drop of PEARSON SAKRIN does the job. And it leaves no bitter after-taste.

So start with new PEARSON SAKRIN Liquid Sweetener today. Carry the regular container to use at lunch and coffee-breaks. Get the super size to keep at home on the table.

69¢ PEARSON SAKRIN equals sweetening power of **OVER 10 LBS. of SUGAR** SAVES YOU 18,144 CALORIES!

$1.49 PEARSON SAKRIN equals sweetening power of **OVER 25 LBS. of SUGAR** SAVES YOU 45,359 CALORIES!

HOW PEARSON SAKRIN CAN SAVE YOU 511 CALORIES DAILY
(in foods where you usually use sugar)

		CALORIES ADDED BY:	
		PEARSON SAKRIN	SUGAR
Breakfast	Fruit Juice	0	16 (1 tsp.)*
	Cereal	0	32 (2 tsp.)
	Coffee or Tea	0	32 (2 tsp.)
Morning Break:	Coffee or Tea	0	32 (2 tsp.)
Lunch:	Fruit Cup	0	32 (2 tsp.)
	Dessert	0	32 (2 tsp.)
	Tea	0	32 (2 tsp.)
Afternoon Break:	Coffee or Tea	0	32 (2 tsp.)
Dinner:	Grapefruit	0	32 (2 tsp.)
	Dessert	0	32 (2 tsp.)
	Coffee or Tea	0	32 (2 tsp.)
Misc. sweetening, incl. mixed drinks, snacks while watching TV, as well as between meals and late evening snacks, etc.		0	175
TOTAL DAILY CALORIES SAVED WITH PEARSON SAKRIN			511

Figure out your daily calorie savings with PEARSON SAKRIN—there may be more or less than above—but every calorie you save helps control weight! **SAVE ONE POUND A WEEK IN SWEETENING CALORIES ALONE!**

SAVES YOU MONEY, TOO!

MAKE THIS TASTE TEST!

Try coffee sweetened with sugar, and coffee sweetened with PEARSON SAKRIN. You can't tell the difference—PEARSON SAKRIN SAVES YOU MANY CALORIES EACH CUP!

GOOD HOUSEKEEPING GUARANTY SEAL!

The world-famous Good Housekeeping Laboratory has studied PEARSON SAKRIN thoroughly and finds it completely effective in providing sweetening with NO Calories, NO Sugar, NO Salt (sodium-free). Therefore PEARSON SAKRIN has earned the Good Housekeeping Seal as a most valuable aid in weight control, reducing diets, other cases, saving hundreds of calories daily.

Guaranteed by Good Housekeeping

REGULAR SIZE—69¢
(Equals sweetness of over 10 lbs. Sugar)

SUPER SIZE—$1.49
(Equals sweetness of over 25 lbs. Sugar)

SAVES YOU CALORIES— SAVES YOU MONEY, TOO!

Free

...In every package of PEARSON SAKRIN—helpful reducing guide: "PEARSON SAKRIN WAY TO SLIMNESS".

PEARSON PHARMACAL CO., INC. LONG ISLAND CITY, N. Y.

Get PEARSON SAKRIN now at Drug Stores, Supermarkets, Grocers, Dept. Stores

Pearson sakrin

LIQUID SWEETENER with exclusive DARAMIN

CANCER UP-DATE

According to a cancer report published in the A.M.A. Journal, despite an increase in life expectancy, research revealed the following grim statistics:

• 36 out of 100 females and 31 out of 100 males born this year will die of cancer.

• Reported cancer cases will increase by over 50% within the next 25 years.

• Cancer occurs at the same rate for men and women, but more men die because of the inaccessibility of the afflicted areas.

• More cases are reported in urban than rural areas while fewer cases are reported among non-whites than whites.

• Sloan-Kettering Institute announces breast cancer may be diagnosed through component found in the blood.

• New sulfur mustard drug appears promising in treatment of Hodgkin's Disease and other forms of lymphatic cancer according to scientists at University of California at San Francisco.

• Abnormal protein found in the blood of cancerous mice.

• The "Smear Technique" found useful in detection of skin cancer.

Cancer Recovery Rate Rises To 50% As A Result Of Early Diagnosis, Surgery And Radiation Therapy.

FDA REPORTS

A national research council set up by the U.S. Food & Drug Administration concluded that poisoning or cancer could result from ingesting of dyes used in coloring food, lipstick and medicines. The report indicated that with its current staffing, it would take the FDA approximately 25 years to test the 116 dyes now certified as harmless.

Doctors Report Link Between Cigarette Smoking And Pulmonary Emphysema.

■ Atlantic City Report Links Lung Cancer to Air Pollution.

■ U.S. Committee of Scientists Reports That Exposure To Even The Smallest Amounts Of Atomic Radiation Harms Not Only The Recipient But Future Generations As Well.

BRAIN STORM...

Temper, Thy Name Be Woman

A study conducted at a New York hospital confirmed what doctors already suspected – that hypertension with its resultant emotional, sometimes dramatic mood swings, is connected to underlying emotional disturbances. Some of their findings:

- More women than men suffer from hypertension;

- Women's need to please prevents expression of emotions which, in addition to mood swings, can manifest in other disorders such as migraine headaches and other physical symptoms.

- Unexpressed emotions are major contributing factors;

Unsure as to exactly how to treat this disorder, one doctor concluded that if the patient has no previous symptoms, the kindest thing he can do is to keep to the information to himself.

Yes Virginia, You Have Pre-Menstrual Blues

A study conducted by English husband and wife team, Drs. Iain and Pamela MacKinnon, presented medical evidence that in the few days preceding menstruation, women experience cellular changes causing them to be more prone to emotional instability including increased capability of committing crimes of violence.

This Could Drive You To Drink...

The Alcoholic Personality Is A Result Of Drinking And Not The Original Cause Of Drinking According to Dr. Robert Fleming, Director Of The Alcoholism Clinic At Boston's Peter Bent Brigham Hospital.

On The Other Hand...

Dr. Giorgio Lolli, Director Of Silkworth Memorial Service At New York's Knicker-bocker Hospital, Believes In A Pre-Alcoholic And Alcoholic Personality With Heredity And Environmental Influences Acting As Contributing Factors.

The American Psychiatric Association issued a warning to its members against the use of tranquilizers as medicine for the relief of everyday tensions and that casual use of such drugs was considered medically unsound and a public danger.

British Neurologist, **Sir Russell Brain**, Applauds *Charles Dickens* For His Impressive Medical Accuracy In Describing The Variety Of Diseases He Inflicted On His Characters.

A SIGNIFICANT RELATIONSHIP IS FOUND BETWEEN PHYSICAL AND MENTAL ILLNESSES.

Mental Patients Account For More Hospital Beds Than All Other Patients Combined.

FIRST PREFRONTAL LOBOTOMY PERFORMED AT GEORGE WASHINGTON UNIVERSITY.

With the rise in diabetes among children, the University of Rochester published its observations as follows:

1 Being underweight, not overweight plays a major role;

2 Eating sweets is not a causal factor;

3 Insulin treatment is necessary in most cases;

4 Flexibility should be practiced for special occasions such as birthday celebrations so that the child does not feel deprived.

> A High-Salt Diet Is Linked To High Blood Pressure

Research Reveals Youngsters With Mouth Or Teeth Deformities Improve Muscle Control By Playing Wind Instruments.

Saliva May Play Important Role In Preventing Tooth Decay According To Dr. C.E. Krapper Of The University Of Alabama Medical Center.

Study Reveals Fluoridated Water Reduces Dental Cavities By At Least 60%.

Bill To Legalize Corneal Transplants Is Introduced In Italy After Successful, Illegal Operation Performed By Distinguished Surgeon, Dr. Cesare Galeazzi. Current Law Forbids Mutilation Of Corpses Within 24 Hours After Death.

PASSINGS

Alfred Kinsey, American Sexologist And Co-Author Of The Book, *Sexual Behavior In The Human Male*, Dies At 62.

Why do so many people work so hard for the money they earn — and then throw it away in taxes they don't really owe?

U. S. Treasury surveys show that millions of Americans overpay their income tax and lose out on hundreds of dollars in savings which are rightfully theirs.

Why overpay your taxes? No matter what your income — no matter how carefully you prepare your return, or have others prepare it for you — you too can save hundreds of dollars this year. The stories on this page represent the many people who *do* save hundreds, and in some cases, thousands of dollars — by having at their fingertips America's most widely-used tax guide — J. K. Lasser's YOUR INCOME TAX. The tax wise person knows that there are many money saving opportunities available *if action is taken before the end of the year.* Act now and save taxes later.

HOMEOWNER: Buying the house put quite a strain on our budget and when the boiler suddenly exploded I thought we were sunk. But then I learned from YOUR INCOME TAX that this loss as well as dozens of other expenses connected with my home were tax deductible. The tax savings alone helped pull us through our toughest year.

SALESMAN: I use my car for selling and do a lot of entertaining. I thought I had deducted everything until Lasser's tax guide showed me 20 deductions I never thought were allowable. It also showed me how to convert an accident I had with my car into a tax saving. I owe my new set of tires to this money-saving book.

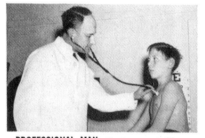

PROFESSIONAL MAN: I've been worried for a long time about the cash I receive and spend without bills to show. Lasser's tax guide showed me a simple way to protect both my pocketbook and my professional reputation.

HOUSEWIFE: Saving on my husband's salary isn't easy. I thought tax returns were a man's job until Lasser's simple tax guide showed me how many of our expenses are deductible—like the clothes I donate to the Salvation Army and my bridge luncheons for local charity. We saved enough for a new washing machine!

BUSINESS EXECUTIVE: I've made good money for years, but have been worried about how to save enough after taxes for retirement and for my family's security. Lasser's tax guide enabled me to add to my after-tax-income, so that I gained increased security—and peace of mind.

YOU MUST SAVE AT LEAST 50 TIMES THE COST OF THE BOOK OR YOU GET YOUR MONEY BACK

THE NEW 1957 "YOUR INCOME TAX" IS GUARANTEED TO NET YOU BIG SAVINGS IN ALL FOUR AREAS OF YOUR PERSONAL FINANCES—your Home, your Pay, your Investments, and your Family Planning Program. Included in its 3157 tested tax-saving ideas are:

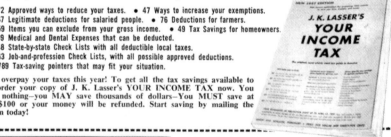

- 372 Approved ways to reduce your taxes.   • 47 Ways to increase your exemptions.
- 567 Legitimate deductions for salaried people.   • 76 Deductions for farmers.
- 459 Items you can exclude from your gross income.   • 49 Tax Savings for homeowners.
- 139 Medical and Dental Expenses that can be deducted.
- 48 State-by-state Check Lists with all deductible local taxes.
- 463 Job-and-profession Check Lists, with all possible approved deductions.
- 1789 Tax-saving pointers that may fit your situation.

Don't overpay your taxes this year! To get all the tax savings available to you, order your copy of J. K. Lasser's YOUR INCOME TAX now. You RISK nothing—you MAY save thousands of dollars—You MUST save at least $100 or your money will be refunded. Start saving by mailing the coupon today!

J. K. LASSER'S YOUR INCOME TAX

SALARIED PEOPLE: For years I've used my employer's report of my earnings and filed a short form return. A few minutes with Lasser's simple guide showed me how I could use the long form to save $123.00.

J. K. Lasser's YOUR BUSINESS TAXES
New 1957 Edition — $1.95

This time saving, tax saving guide gives line by line instructions for all tax forms for every type of business. In addition, it contains hundreds of tax saving ideas for sole proprietors, partnerships, corporations, etc. Specially designed to help all those who fill out tax returns for businesses.

Simon and Schuster, Publishers, New York

MAIL THIS GUARANTEE COUPON TODAY AND RECEIVE FREE FILLED-IN TAX FORMS.

SPECIAL FREE BONUS: Filled-In 1956 Tax Forms—To give you every possible tax saving—and to save you time and trouble —you will also receive a 16-page booklet of sample 1956 tax forms, completely filled in for your guidance. This is yours to keep, even if you return the 1957 YOUR INCOME TAX for refund.

☐ *Also send me Lasser's YOUR BUSINESS TAXES at $1.95, for which payment is enclosed. If not entirely satisfied, I can return the book within two weeks for full refund.*

To Your Bookseller, or
SIMON AND SCHUSTER, Publishers, Tax Dept. T-36
630 Fifth Avenue, New York 20, N. Y.
  Rush me .... copies of the new 1957 J. K. Lasser YOUR INCOME TAX. I enclose $1.95 per copy. If the book does not save me at least $100, I may return it for refund any time up to April 16, 1957.

NAME_____
  (Please Print)
ADDRESS_____
CITY_____ZONE____STATE_____

132

It's a Living

3% Federal Reserve Board And Federal Deposit Insurance Corp. Announce U.S. Commercial Banks Will Be Allowed To Pay A Maximum 3% Interest Rate On Savings Deposits Effective January 1, 1957.

LONG DISTANCE
TELEPHONE RATES*

San Francisco to Washington, D.C. ...	$2.00
Milwaukee to New York	1.20
Dallas to Denver	1.10
Chicago to Buffalo	.95
New York to Boston	.55
Pittsburgh to Cleveland	.45

First 3 minutes, evenings and Sundays

WALL STREET

AMERICAN TELEPHONE AND TELEGRAPH COMPANY

Announces Plans To Offer 5,750,000 Shares Of Common Stock To Its Shareholders, Making It The Largest Common Stock Offering In History.

U.S. Antitrust Suit Against American Telephone And Telegraph Settled By Consent Decree – Patents Open To All Applicants.

The Ford Foundation Makes First PublicOffering Of Its Stock.

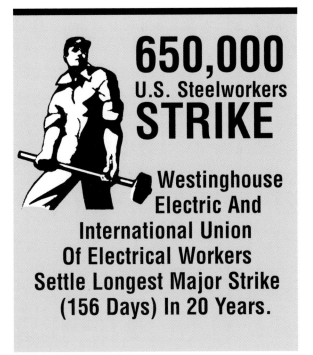

650,000
U.S. Steelworkers
STRIKE

Westinghouse Electric And International Union Of Electrical Workers Settle Longest Major Strike (156 Days) In 20 Years.

ELECTRONICS U.S.
FIFTH LARGEST INDUSTRY

The Price That Was

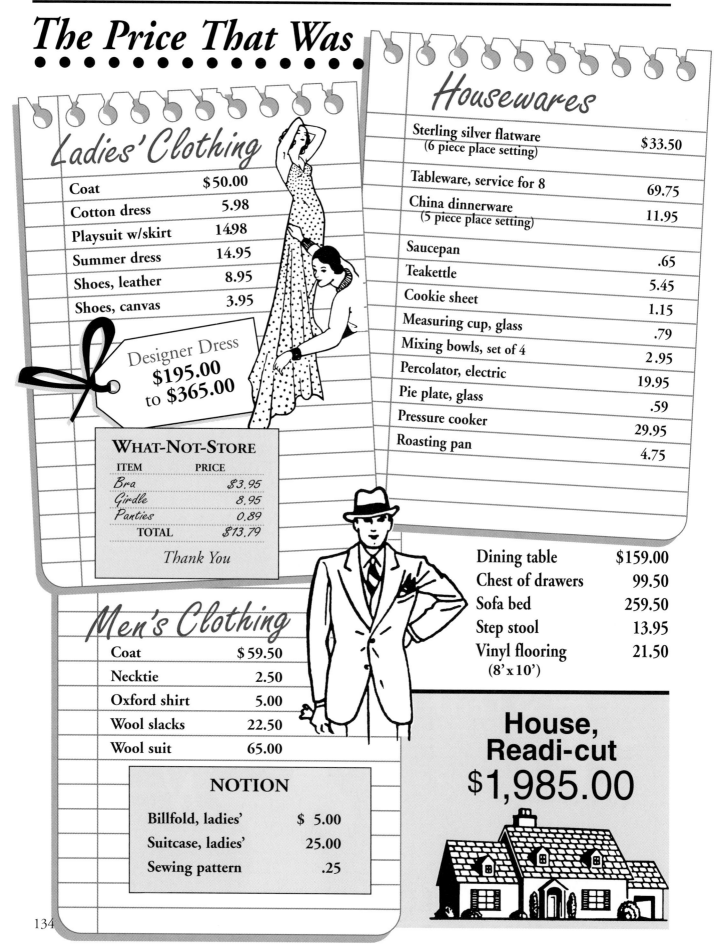

Ladies' Clothing

Coat	$50.00
Cotton dress	5.98
Playsuit w/skirt	14.98
Summer dress	14.95
Shoes, leather	8.95
Shoes, canvas	3.95

Designer Dress
$195.00 to $365.00

WHAT-NOT-STORE

ITEM	PRICE
Bra	$3.95
Girdle	8.95
Panties	0.89
TOTAL	$13.79

Thank You

Housewares

Sterling silver flatware (6 piece place setting)	$33.50
Tableware, service for 8	69.75
China dinnerware (5 piece place setting)	11.95
Saucepan	.65
Teakettle	5.45
Cookie sheet	1.15
Measuring cup, glass	.79
Mixing bowls, set of 4	2.95
Percolator, electric	19.95
Pie plate, glass	.59
Pressure cooker	29.95
Roasting pan	4.75

Dining table	$159.00
Chest of drawers	99.50
Sofa bed	259.50
Step stool	13.95
Vinyl flooring (8' x 10')	21.50

Men's Clothing

Coat	$59.50
Necktie	2.50
Oxford shirt	5.00
Wool slacks	22.50
Wool suit	65.00

NOTION

Billfold, ladies'	$ 5.00
Suitcase, ladies'	25.00
Sewing pattern	.25

House, Readi-cut
$1,985.00

Mr. and Mrs. Potato-Head

$1.98

IT'S LIQUID—goes to work faster

IT'S POWERFUL—unites the powers of several *proved* ingredients

IT'S COMPLETE—takes the place of nose spray, antihistamine, gargle, cough syrup, chest rub and pain reliever

ONLY $100

coldene
THE LIQUID
COLD MEDICINE

Copyright 1956
Pharma-Craft Company
Batavia, Illinois

Jet Jumper

$4.95
ages 4-8

$6.95
ages 9-16

AMF Junior Roadmaster

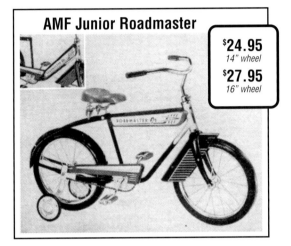

$24.95
14" wheel

$27.95
16" wheel

AVERAGE YEARLY DRIVING COSTS FOR A FAMILY OF FOUR FOR 15,000 MILES

Depreciation	$481.33
Gasoline & Oil	348.00
Insurance	104.39
License Fees	16.86
Maintenance	111.00
Tires	76.50

PASSINGS

THOMAS J. WATSON,
Chairman Of The Board Of IBM,
Dies At 82.

WILLIAM BOEING,
Pioneer In Aircraft Technology,
Dies At 74.

CLARENCE BIRDSEYE,
Inventor Of Quick Freezing Process
For Foods, Dies At 69.

CHARLES EDWARD MERRILL,
Founder Of Merrill Lynch, Started Safeway
Stores And Family Circle Magazine,
Dies At 70.

SAMUEL A. LERNER,
Founder Of Lerner Stores, Dies At 72.

HARRY FORD SINCLAIR,
Founder Of Sinclair Oil Corp., Dies At 80.

MARSHALL FIELD III,
Heir To Chicago Store Millions,
Dies at 63.

By **JUDY BOND**. Left: Nylon georgette ombré print in grey, green, red, navy, toast. Right: Nylon tricot in white, pink, blue, natural. Sizes 32 to 38. Each about $6. (Also by Judy Bond, Ltd., in Canada.)

without a care in the world

Gift-minded? These care-free blouses of 100% Du Pont nylon will delight every lady on your list
—*including yourself!* One is gentle nylon georgette, dancing with dots. The other is nylon tricot,
trimmed with tinsel and lit with lace. And besides all their fashionable blessings—they wash
divinely and dry quickly to first-day freshness. Available at fine stores everywhere.

DU PONT

REG. U.S. PAT. OFF.

BETTER THINGS FOR BETTER LIVING... *THROUGH CHEMISTRY*

Du Pont makes nylon fiber, does not make the fabrics or blouses shown here.

DU PONT NYLON

136

Fashion

The Teen Look

girls

- Oversized men's shirt with rolled up jeans
- Penny loafers or black-and-white saddle shoes
- Hair: ponytail

boys

- Blue jeans with penny loafers or black-and-white saddle shoes
- Hair: the Elvis Presley look – greasy ducktail and sideburns
- Ivy League Look

PASSINGS

HATTIE CARNEGIE, Designer To The Rich And Famous, Dies At 69 Of Cancer.

I'll take romance...

The return to the "Romantic Look" brings grace, charm and beauty to women's fashion this year with designer collections incorporating yards and yards of extravagant clinging or floating fabrics like white sheer silk dresses embroidered in pink and gold or pastel dotted organdy gowns with winged sleeves, trimmed with pink ribbons and roses on the bodice. The silhouette is softened through the use of draping and a profusion of color is generously used, moving away from stark simplicity to the visual opulence brought to life by the stunning costumes seen in "My Fair Lady" reflecting the late Edwardian period (1906-1912).

Capes are seen everywhere – with collars, hoods, or shawls, and some trimmed with that new status symbol fur – mink.

The World's Beautiful Women

Tenley Albright

Anita Ekberg

Greta Garbo

Ava Gardner

Grace Kelly

Gina Lollobrigida

Anna Magnani

Maharanee of Jaipur

Kim Novak

Grace Paley

Sharon Kay Ritchie

Eva Marie Saint

Elizabeth Taylor

Jeanne Vanderbilt

THE BASICS OF AN ELEGANT WARDROBE
Simplicity Is The Key

1. Three Basic Elements
   a. A Suit
   b. A Sheath
   c. A Narrow, Décolleté Cocktail Dress
2. Real Jewels Or Copies Of Old Ones
3. Contrasting Colors For Bags & Hats
4. Slender Heels, Not Too High
5. Gloves (8-buttons vs. Shorter Length)

The **Don Loper** Collection

Designer Don Loper escorts his favorite model, Marilyn, for a day at the Beverly Hills Hotel. She wears one of his creations – a two-piece suit designed to travel.

A mandarin ensemble over blue taffeta set off with a glamorous harlequin bow.

Another piece in his collection is this gold linen ensemble with polka dot silk and mandarin side slit coat accessorized with a fishnet basket purse and a large piped straw cartwheel hat.

This evening gown in the new flamenco length is called "Symphony" and is made of re-embroidered mauve lace with a graceful, flowing draped sash panel.

And for the hourglass look, here's Loper's "Can-Can" evening gown, handpainted lace over layers of tulle.

MISSES' NOVELTY FANCY TOPS Cuddly soft, festive cardigans aglitter with merry tinsel, velveray, rhinestones, and bouncy flower trims. Bright gift ideas. Christmasy whites, pastels. Small, medium, large. **1.89**

MISSES' SMART COSTUME MAKERS IN THREE MOODS Nylon or dacron batiste blouses with dress-up trims. **2.89** Wool jersey, sparkling trims, smart details. **3.89** *4.98 value* Orlon cardigan, lurex collar, rhinestones. **4.89** *5.98 value*

GIRLS' HI-BULK ORLON FASHION CARDIGANS Crew or mock turtle necklines prettied with lace flower petals, daisies, appliqued pansies and make-believe jewels. Holiday red, white, pink, turquoise. 7-14. **2.89**

Christmastime or anytime...

your money buys _more_ at ROBERT HALL!

This Christmas Robert Hall brings you thousands of colorful, lasting gifts for the whole family... at 20% to 40% savings! Our low overhead stretches your clothing dollar twelve months of the year... 'specially now. Robert Hall does it this way: no high rents, no middlemen, no fancy fixtures or window displays, no credit losses... those costly extras that add nothing to quality or value. This Christmas pay less, give more. Bring your Santa list to Robert Hall! **YOU'LL SAVE 20% TO 40%**

Robert Hall

SEE OPPOSITE PAGE FOR NEAREST LOCATION

A DIVISION OF THE UNITED MERCHANTS & MFRS.

MEN'S ALL WOOL SPORTSCOATS Handsome splash weaves, overplaids, tweeds. **19.95** *$25 value* **ALL WOOL FLANNEL SLACKS** Costly fabrics, expert tailoring. Popular tones. **8.95** *12.95 value*

MEN'S WARM MELTON SUBURBAN COATS Nobby-look melton, so handsome it can be worn anywhere. Deluxe tailoring with cash pocket and quilted lining. **15.95** *$21 value*

BOYS' QUILT LINED SUBURBANS AND PARKAS Melton suburban coats in solids, fibrenes. 6-18. Parkas in two-tone wool fleece or melton. Sizes 4-10. **10.99** *$13 value*

LITTLE MISS 3 PC. JUMPER DRESS SETS Dress, nylon blouse, tote. 3-6x. **3.89** *3.98 value* **3 PC. COORDINATE SWEATER SETS** Knit top & circle skirt, bag. 3-6x. **3.89** *4.98 value*

LADIES' HOODED CAR COATS Cotton sateen in Loden style with big collar that converts to hood. Warm 12 oz. quilted lining. Sizes 8-18. **9.66** *Terrific buy!*

MISSES' WOOL KNIT 2 PC. DRESS Smart fashion as separates or as a dress. Snowy angora collars, dolman sleeve top. Rib effect skirt. Black, aqua, pink, beige. 10-18. **11.89** *14.95 value*

CHOOSE HIS GIFT FROM THIS TRIO OF MEN'S OUTDOOR JACKETS *left:* Imported suede leather, knit trim, quilt-lined. **16.95** *22.95 value* *center:* Quilt-lined gabardine (rayon-nylon) surcoat, welt detail. **9.95** *$13 value* *right:* Quilt-lined woolen melton blouse jacket, zipper front. **9.95** *$13 value*

LADIES' WASHABLE QUILTED GIFT DUSTER Gay printed acetate in soft blue or pink. Gracefully flared, piped. 12-20. **3.89** *4.98 value*

GIFTS WITH A FLARE! MISSES' FELT SKIRTS Full circle felts in solids and iridescents. Felts flared wide with 30 gores. Black, charcoal gray and new fashion hues. 22-30. **4.89** *5.98 value*

EVERY BOY CAN USE EXTRA SLACKS Rayon-dacron gabardines, cotton corduroys, rayon fancies. 8-18. **3.99** *$5 value* Fine all wool flannels. 4-10. **4.69** *$6 value*

BOYS' COLORFUL NOVELTY GIFT SETS 3.89 each *$5 values* Gay blade's corduroy slack, fancy vest, bow-tie. 3-6x. Westerner, fringed and jewelled, in Sanforized cotton twill. 4-10. "Ivy" leaguer's plaid or striped button-down shirt, cotton sheen pants. 3-8. Real boys' gifts.

COPR. 1956 ROBERT HALL CLOTHES.

MAKE THIS AN ACME

Cowboy Boot Christmas

Acme Cowboy Boots have been awarded the Parents' Magazine Seal of Commendation.

The most wanted gift of all!

Dreams come true in these colorful Acme Cowboy Boots . . . bringing endless hours of pleasure to those who believe in the exciting world of the glamorous Old West! If you want the wonderful thrill of giving exactly what they want . . . here's your answer! Fine leathers and Acme craftsmanship in every pair! Built for rough, tough, comfortable wear! What youngster can resist them! At such low cost, what parent can deny them! See them now . . . make your selection now . . . Acme Cowboy Boots!

Fine boots cost less than you think!

MOST STYLES PRICED AT . . .
Infants'—$3.95 to $6.95
Boys' and Girls'—$5.95 to $12.95
Ladies' and Men's—$12.95 to $22.50

WORLD'S MOST POPULAR COWBOY BOOTS
ACME BOOT COMPANY, Inc., Clarksville, Tenn.

141

CHRISTIAN DIOR FASHION

The Dior collection features a return to the picture hat.

A hint of Casablanca in this multi-colored striped silk with its hood and flowing lines.

This sports outfit is a brilliant red linen which buttons from neckline to hemline.

HELENA BARBIERI
UNVEILS FEMININE EVENING WEAR

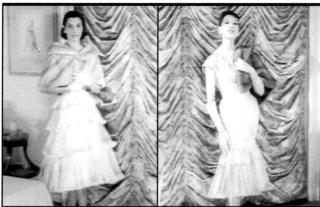

A lace and embroidered sheer cocktail creation is set off with a mutation mink.

The Dresden figurine look is captured in this beautiful pin-tucked sheer that folds into a cascade of pleats topped off with an autumn haze capelet.

This wraparound jacket lined with millium will insure staying cool.

Pink brocade evening coats are accented by deep pockets, bows, and mauve lining.

Sparkling earrings and bracelet make this the height of fashion.

1956 ADVERTISEMENT

The new, new, new...

"Lady Ronson"
ELECTRIC SHAVER

Keeps your legs and underarms smooth as slipper satin...and it's fun to use!

How *ridiculous* to risk old-fashioned razors that leave nasty little nicks, or razor-burned skin! It's so safe and *simple* to "defuzz" with "LADY RONSON", the chic little shaver with *two sides:* one to give legs a slipper-satin finish...one to keep underarms smooth as a baby's! And with "LADY RONSON", you shave *far less frequently,* stay hair-free days *longer!* You'll adore it!

It's the glamour gift of the year!

○ *Blush Pink*
◐ *Blue Heaven*
○ *Turquoise*
● *Black Magic*

Set with a make-believe diamond!

14⁹⁵
(complete with case)

RONSON® *maker of the world's greatest lighters and electric shavers*

COSTUME TINA LESER · RONSON CORPORATION NEWARK 2 N J · TORONTO ONT · LONDON ENG

144

HAVING YOUR EASTER HAT AND EATING IT TOO!

Not only do these Easter bonnets look delicious, they are delicious as the pastry chef whipped them up out of powdered sugar and egg whites.

How many calories do you suppose are in this little bonnet?

145

Jantzen Kharafleece Sweaters

The luxury in the fabric is *Vicara*

BRAND ZEIN FIBERS

Getting a rush on every campus—fall's new Kharafleece sweaters lavishly enriched with lush *Vicara* fiber. Glad news you may not find in a textbook—not only does this luxury fiber bring a soft beauty to the blend, it also keeps you blissfully comfortable! Because *Vicara* fiber is absorbent, you never have that unpleasant cold and clammy feeling. Your new Kharafleece sweater washes easier...no blocking, no shrinking, no stretching. And it resists soiling longer... *Vicara* fiber is anti-static, simply doesn't attract lint or dirt. Its gentle, well-bred good looks will last...there'll be no unsightly matting, no "fuzzing up". Most of all, you'll revel in its rich texture, a heavenly touch that sweaters never had before...a precious gift of luxury that only *Vicara* fiber bestows on the nicest sweaters you'll ever own. Remember the name: Kharafleece sweaters by Jantzen!

Jantzen Kharafleece knitwear is yours in an opulent range of colors at fine stores everywhere. Hand-washable, mothproof, wrinkle-resistant. Girl's sweater, about 11.00. Skirt, about 14.00. Men's sweaters, about 12.00. The golfer shirt (about 13.00) and sheath dress (about 30.00) are also in wonderful Kharafleece. Vicara brand zein fibers are made by Virginia-Carolina Chemical Corporation 99 Park Avenue, New York 16, New York

Sports

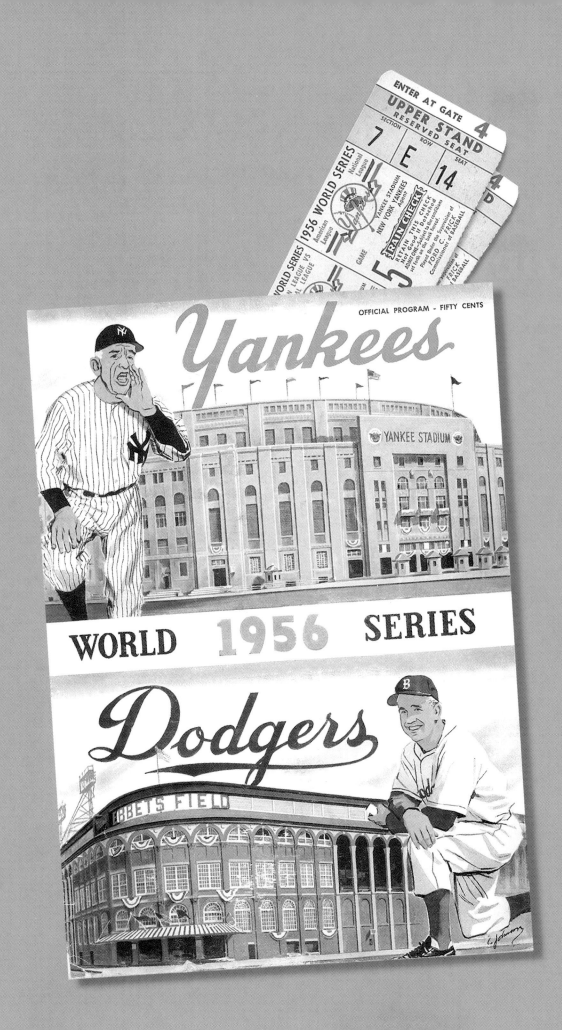

Baseball

THOUSANDS OF FANS GATHER TO CHEER THEIR FAVORITE TEAM.

YANKEES AND DODGERS BATTLE FOR WORLD SERIES CROWN

Mickey Mantle climaxes the winning season capturing the triple crown.

A thrilling moment for the victorious Yankees.

Yankee pitcher Don Larsen makes baseball history.

Baseball Hall Of Famer
CONNIE MACK Dies

Connie will be remembered not only for his baseball skills but for the character and integrity he typified.

Cornelius McGillicuddy, known throughout his 70-year baseball career as Connie Mack, is pictured with Babe Ruth and other Hall of Famers.

WHAT DO YA MEAN YOU DIDN'T LIKE THAT CATCH!

Boston Red Sox's **Ted Williams** Fined $5,000 After He Spit At Fans And Reporters During A Game Played Against The Yankees.

Comedy Team **Abbott** & **Costello's** **"Who's On First"** Baseball Routine Is Enshrined In Baseball Hall Of Fame.

Rookie Of The Year:

LOU APARICIO
(Chicago White Sox)

FRANK ROBINSON
(Cincinnati Redlegs)

Player Of The Year:

MICKEY MANTLE

DALE LONG, Pittsburgh First Baseman, Sets Major League Record By Hitting A Home Run In Eight Consecutive Games.

DON LARSEN Of The New York Yankees, Pitches The First Perfect Major League Baseball Game In 34 Years And The First No-Hit Game In World Series History.

NEW YORK YANKEES
Take Their 17th World Series Victory By Beating Brooklyn 4-3.

Baseball's Yearly Schedule Is Set In Braille For The First Time, Appearing In The May 7 Issue Of The "Weekly News," The Only Newspaper For The Blind In The English-Speaking World.

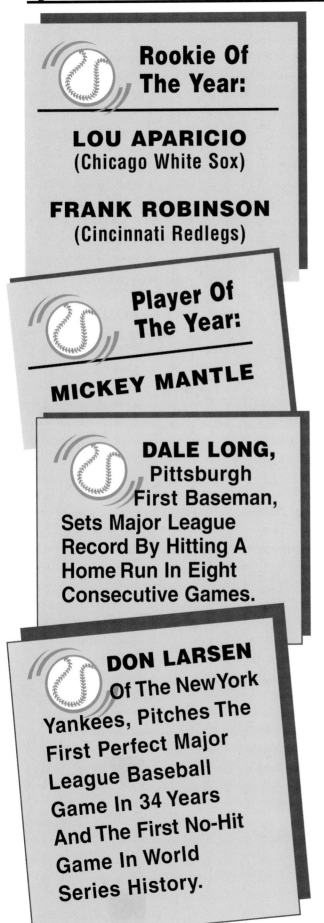

THE BEL AIR BEAUVILLE—*4 doors, 9 passengers, interior finish in washable vinyl and nylon-faced pattern cloth.*

Seats a whole baseball team

It's one of __6__ sprightly

THE "TWO-TEN" HANDYMAN
2 doors, 6 passengers, all-vinyl interior.

THE DISTINCTIVE, LUXURIOUS NOMAD
2 doors, 6 passengers.

THE "TWO-TEN" TOWNSMAN
4 doors, 6 passengers, loads of cargo space.

In place of baseball players, of course, it could be other people. Friends of yours, for instance, assorted small fry, or visiting dignitaries.

Anyway, there's room for 3 on each seat, 9 in all. (A separate section of the center seat folds down to allow rear seat passengers to get in and out easily and gracefully.) And there's even space left over for baseball bats or baggage.

If you're joining the fast-growing station wagon family, be sure to look these new Chevrolets over. They're very good looking, as you see. All of them have fine, sturdy and quiet Fisher Bodies. All offer you an engine choice of V8 or 6, and all the power features anybody would want. And all of them pack Chevrolet's special brand of performance that breaks records on Pikes Peak and makes your own driving easier, safer and more pleasant.

Color and interior choices are wide, practical and unusually handsome. We'll be happy to help you make your selection.

SEE YOUR CHEVROLET DEALER

beautifully!

new Chevrolet station wagons

THE "ONE-FIFTY" HANDYMAN
2 doors, 6 passengers, versatile and thrifty.

THE "TWO-TEN" BEAUVILLE
4 doors, 9 passengers.

CHEVROLET

Traffic-test it— it's a beautiful thing to handle!

153

FOOTBALL

EAST MEETS WEST IN PRO BOWL GAME

Top players in the National League meet in the Pro Bowl Game. Christiansen of the Lions sets the stage with a run back of 103 yards.

Christiansen scores a touchdown for the West.

LeBaron of the Redskins throws a pass that is intercepted by Jim David of the West All-Stars.

Hearst scores — making the final score East 31, West 30.

MICHIGAN STATE Beats UCLA 17-14 In Rose Bowl Competition.

★★★★★★★★★★

Army And Navy Tie 7-7 In Philadelphia.

★★★★★★★★★★

Heisman Trophy Winner: PAUL HORNUNG (Notre Dame Quarterback)

Best U.S. College Football Team: **OKLAHOMA**

Football Coach Of The Year: **BOWDEN WYATT**, University Of Tennessee

New York Giants Beat Chicago Bears 47-7, Winning NFL Championship.

Basketball

Philadelphia Warriors Beat Fort Wayne Pistons 4-1 For NBA Championship.

San Francisco Whips Iowa 83-71, Winning NCAA Championship

6'9" Bill Russell Becomes A Boston Celtic And Marries Rose Swisher In Oakland, California.

Most Valuable Player: Bob Pettit (St. Louis Hawks)

Rookie Of The Year: Maurice Stokes (Rochester Royals)

Son And Grandson Of Derby Winners

Uphold The Family Honor

HORSE RACING

RACING FORM

In one of the richest derbies ever, and one of the most thrilling in the history of the Kentucky classic, D. Erb rides "Needles" to victory, moving from 16th place. "Needles" also wins the Belmont Stakes.

GOLF MASTERS
GOLF TOURNAMENT IN AUGUSTA, GA

Ken Venturi's lead by 8 strokes collapses in the final round as rival Jack Burke climaxes a great rally to hole out one stroke, winning the title and $6,000 purse.

Venturi congratulates Burke after a stunning match.

Burke puts on the green coat of victory.

SPECTATORS GATHER TO WATCH THE COMPETITION BETWEEN KEN VENTURI AND JACK BURKE.

The Great Babe Zaharias Dies

The world mourns the passing of Babe Didrikson Zaharias, considered to be the greatest woman athlete of all time.

Babe's warm-hearted sportsmanship never failed during her gallant 3-year fight against cancer.

champions

U.S. OPEN
CARY MIDDLECOFF

MASTERS
JACK BURKE

BRITISH OPEN
PETER THOMSON

NATIONAL AMATEUR GOLF

In the National Amateur Tournament held at Lake Forest, defending title holder Harvey Ward holed out five and four to become the first two-time amateur champ in 21 years.

Indy 500-Mile Memorial Day Classic

A series of chilling accidents knock out 12 cars from the race, but fortunately there is no loss of life.

33 cars line up for start of the annual classic.

Red-headed Pat Flaherty emerges the victor.

So Refreshing!
Never bitter - never harsh!

No other beer refreshes like Schlitz, nor gives such satisfaction and pleasure. Here is a beer so fine it made a city famous!

Brewed for quality, never for price, Schlitz is preferred (and bought) by more people than any other beer, at *any* price.

THE BEER THAT MADE MILWAUKEE FAMOUS

© 1956—Jos. Schlitz Brewing Company, Milwaukee, Wis. Brooklyn, N. Y., Los Angeles, Calif.

Diving Trials

Pat McCormick takes top high diving spot and goes on to win at the Summer Olympics in Melbourne.

Barbara Sue Gilders takes second place.

Jeanne Stunyo finishes in third place.

1956 SUMMER OLYMPIC GAMES OPENED BY DUKE OF EDINBURGH IN MELBOURNE, AUSTRALIA.

WINNERS

MEN'S TRACK & FIELD

100 Meter Run:
Robert Morrow (USA)

400 Meter Run:
Charles Jenkins (USA)

1500 Meter Run:
Ron Delany (Ireland)

5000 Meter Run:
Vladimir Kuts (USSR)

High Jump:
Charles Dumas (USA)

Pole Vault:
Robert Richards (USA)

WOMEN'S SWIMMING

100 Meter Freestyle:	Dawn Fraser (Australia)
400 Meter Freestyle:	Lorraine Crapp (Australia)
100 Meter Butterfly:	Shelley Mann (USA)
Platform Diving:	Patricia McCormick (USA)
Springboard Diving:	Patricia McCormick (USA)

SHELLEY MANN

FAMOUS BIRTHS

LARRY BIRD

JOE MONTANA

BJORN BORG

SUGAR RAY LEONARD

MARTINA NAVRATILOVA

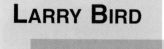

Ten horses of the United States Olympic Jumping Team are loaded aboard a trans-Atlantic plane for their trip to Stockholm for the June competition.

The valuable steeds are secured in their stalls for a long 15-hour flight.

The equestrian team gets ready to board with high hopes of bringing home an Olympic victory.

OLYMPIC STEEPLECHASE TRIALS HELD OUTSIDE OF STOCKHOLM

Horses and riders representing 19 nations gather to compete in the Olympic steeplechase on a rain-drenched, perilous 22-mile course.

45 official hazards send six riders to the hospital with 11 teams failing to finish.

One badly injured horse had to be destroyed in this memorable but not inspiring sport event.

WINTER OLYMPICS

AMERICA SWEEPS ARTISTIC EVENTS IN WINTER OLYMPICS HELD IN CORTINA D'AMPEZZO, ITALY

Hayes Alan Jenkins gives a stylistic performance on the ice.

Tenley Albright, still in pain from a recent leg injury, shows courage to match her gracefulness.

The Champions:
Hayes Alan Jenkins and Tenley Albright.

With Soviet athletes dominating the Winter Olympics, the 500 meter speed skating is an easy win for the Iron Curtain Team.

Austria's domination was visible on the giant slalom with Tony Sailer easily taking the trail that plummets downward for almost two miles through 69 gates with a vertical drop of one mile to the finish line, winning the gold medal.

Tony Sailer wins the slalom, giant slalom and the downhill on one of Europe's toughest, trickiest slopes.

WINNERS

FIGURE SKATING:
  Men's: *Hayes Alan Jenkins (USA)*
  Women's: *Tenley Albright (USA)*
  Pairs: *Elisabeth Schwartz & Kurt Oppelt (Austria)*

SPEED SKATING:
  Men's 500 Meters: *Evgeniy Grishin (USSR)*
  Men's 10,000 Meters: *Sigvard Ericsson (Sweden)*

ALPINE SKIING:
  Men's Downhill: *Anton Sailer (Austria)*
  Women's Downhill: *Madeleine Berthod (Switzerland)*

Track & Field

John Landy (left) congratulates Jim Bailey after his historic run.

Track and field history is made in Los Angeles Coliseum as Australia's John Landy, making his American debut, is upset by fellow Aussie Jim Bailey in a sensational race.

First 4-Minute Mile Run In The United States

Charlie Dumas, 19, clears the 7-foot mark in the high jump, an accomplishment comparable to the first 4-minute mile.

ICE SKATING

WORLD CHAMPIONSHIP

Men: *Hayes Alan Jenkins (U.S.)*
Women: *Carol Heiss (U.S.)*

U.S. NATIONAL

MEN: *Hayes Alan Jenkins*
WOMEN: *Tenley Albright*

CANADIAN NATIONAL

MEN: *Charles Snelling*
WOMEN: *Carole Jane Pachl*

ICE BOAT RACING

Boats line up for the annual regatta sponsored by the Northwestern Ice Yacht Association on Lake Geneva, Wisconsin.

Sailing across the ice, the sailing sleighs reach speeds of up to 50 miles per hour with some ice boats hitting record speeds of over 100 miles per hour.

HOCKEY
Montreal Canadiens Beat Detroit Red Wings 4-1 For Stanley Cup Championship

kayak

sea-going slalom in Germany

The quaint old mountain village of Monschau near the Belgian border is the site of the first seagoing slalom of the season.

The surging current slams this athlete into a wall.

Kayak skippers from five nations compete in the cold, rough waters.

The chilled but thrilled winners.

Austrian and Polish bikers compete in Vienna.

20,000 horrified fans watch as luck runs out for one of the daredevils who meets a fiery death after crashing into another biker wedging himself in a stairwell.

The second biker crawls to safety and the race continues.

Motorcycle Racing

The Annual Hill Climb Sponsored By The Lewis & Clark Motorcycle Club Gets Under Way In Lewiston, Idaho.

CHAMPIONS

TOUR DE FRANCE
Roger Walkowiak

ATHLETE OF THE YEAR

Male	Female
Mickey Mantle (Baseball)	**Pat McCormick** (Diving)

tennis

Althea Gibson, First Black Player To Tour The Major World Amateur Tennis Circuit, Places Second In Women's Singles Tennis Championship At Forest Hills, NY After Capturing Titles In France, Italy And Great Britain.

TENNIS CHAMPIONS

U.S. Lawn Tennis:

Men's Singles
Ken Rosewall

Women's Singles
Shirley Fry

Wimbledon:

Men
Lew Hoad (vs. Ken Rosewall)

Women
Shirley Fry (vs. Angela Buxton)

Feel fresh again fast!

(RICHardson's cool, rich, zippy flavor does it)

RICHardson
ROOT BEER
Rich in flavor

STRAWBERRY
TOPPING

Now--enjoy 'em at home

Your favorite soda fountain milk shakes, sundaes, sodas in five take-home flavors!

Chocolate • Butterscotch • Strawberry • Pineapple • Walnut

RICHardson Corporation
Rochester 3, N.Y.

All About Bulls

According to a New York City psychoanalyst, bull-fighting is a Freudian unconscious acting out of the Oedipean battle between father and son for sexual supremacy. So, if you thought the sport was about pageantry, skill, danger and a lot of gore, get yourself to the nearest analyst's couch!

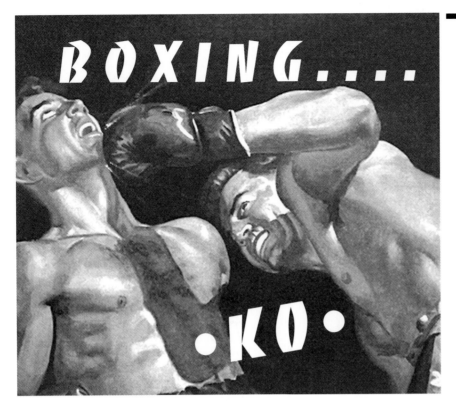

Rocky Marciano Retires Undefeated Heavyweight Champion Of The World After Winning All 46 Of His Pro Fights, 43 Of Which Were Knockouts.

Floyd Patterson (21) Knocks Out Archie Moore In Title Fight, Becoming Youngest Boxer To Win Heavyweight Crown.

Johnny Saxton Beats Carmen Basilio And Regains The World Welterweight Title.

CHESS

John Hudson, AAF Navigator, Wins U.S. Chess Federation Amateur Title Tournament.

AUTO RACING
Britain's Stirling Moss Wins Grand Prix Of Monaco Driving A Maserati.

PARACHUTING

French Fashion Model, Colette Duval, Breaks Her Own Women's World Record In Free-Fall Parachute Jump, Dropping 34,000 Ft. From A Plane Over Rio de Janeiro Before Opening Her Chute.

ROWING

Cornell Wins The Eastern Association Of Rowing Colleges Sprint Race.

BADMINTON

U.S. OPEN CHAMPIONSHIP

Men's Singles: Finn Kobbero, Denmark

Women's Singles: Judy Devlin, USA

VOLLEYBALL

Embarcadero (San Francisco) Wins U.S. Masters Title. U.C.L.A. Wins Collegiate Title

PASSINGS

GRACE REIDY COMISKEY, president of Chicago White Sox (*1st woman president in American League*), dies at 62.

Clarence "Ginger" Beaumont, major league outfielder, first man to bat in a World Series game (1903), dies at 79.

FLICKBACK has the perfect gift to bring a nostalgic smile to the lips of anyone celebrating a birthday, anniversary or reunion. Or, why not treat yourself?

Your friend or loved one will be delighted to receive the original **FLICKBACK**, *the colorful DVD Gift Card full of stories and pictures from their fabulous year. The collector's DVD presents entertaining highlights featuring the people and events that made their year special. A dedication page conveys your personal message and an envelope is included for mailing.*

WHAT A YEAR IT WAS! *is a lavish, 176-page hardcover "scrapbook" packed with stories, photos and artwork detailing the movies, music, shows, sports, fashion, news, people, places and events that make a year unique and memorable. A special dedication page completes a truly personal yearbook gift which will be treasured for years to come.*

Products available for years 1929 through 1974.

Video products are also available in vhs format.

Explore our website or call to find a **FLICKBACK** retailer near you.

www. **FLICKBACK** .com

(800) 541-3533